Forward

This book was created to provide a quick and easy daily dose of wisdom. The inspiration to write this book came from many sources, from ancient writings, religious contexts, mediumship and modern philosophy.

WizzWords can be picked up any time and flicked through randomly or followed throughout the year over 365 days.

It is designed to provoke a deeper, more profound understanding of truth and who we are on our pathway to enlightenment.

May it help to lift the veil of illusion, to clear the way to self-realisation.

April 2017

Day 1

Open Parachute

Your mind is like a parachute……better to keep it open.

Day 2

Universal Connection

We are all connected to the universe and to each other.

Day 3

Clean Windows

Clean the windows of your mind and you will be able to see more clearly.

Day 4

Time and Distance

Time is a great healer. A mountain appears to become the size of a molehill as you travel further away from it.

Day 5

To infinity and beyond.

Astronomers are seeing distant galaxies that took billions of years for the light to reach us on Earth. But what's beyond that? Atoms might have seemed the smallest unit of matter but then we discovered Quarks. But what's smaller than that? We are surrounded by unseen radiation like Gamma, X and Neutron. What else surrounds us that we are unable to detect? Surely our lives are a moving point somewhere between infinity and beyond.

Day 6

Put it into practice.

Don't spend too much time tuning your instrument, lest you never get time to play it.

Day 7

Love conquers all.

Love is unconditional and universal. It is not jealousy, infatuation or judgemental. It breaks through all conflict between individuals, religions, races and countries.

Day 8

Tomorrow never comes.

Why hope for a better tomorrow when you can live for today.

Day 9

Less is more.

In resting the mind to become quieter, there is more understanding.

Day 10

Give your attention to where you are going.

Best not think too much about the past. If you drive a car looking through the rear-view window, you will surely crash.

Day 11

Talking tongues

Your tongue is like the rudder of a boat; it will steer you through life. Better to think about where you want to go before engaging it.

Day 12

The speed of light.

Look into the sky on a clear night and see the distant stars. Owing to the speed of light they all represent different points in time. So there's nothing up there that represents the present moment.

Day 13

Law of Attraction

If you feel bored then life will be boring. If you are judgemental then you will live in a world of criticism. If you feel negative then you will attract negativity. Why not do something interesting, stop judging, smile, feel grateful for what you have and the world will be a wonderful place live.

Day 14

Rich in friends

You can be wealthy but poor in friends. You can also be poor but rich in friends.

Day 15

Know thyself

It is better to go nowhere and fully know yourself than it is to travel the world, yet understand nothing.

Day 16

The hardest thing to do is to do nothing.

We fill our minds with countless thoughts, fantasies, going over past events, which shape our feelings for good or for bad.

The challenge is to be still in the mind for a few minutes. How difficult it is to do the simplest thing.

Day 17

Perfect World.

Conflict arises in our minds when we expect perfection only to find that we live in an imperfect world.

Day 18

Wabi-Sabi

There is beauty in imperfection.

Day 19

Alone : All - One

There's a reason why the word 'alone' is derived from the words 'all one'. Sometimes we need to be alone to feel all at one with ourselves.

Day 20

<u>An eye for an eye.</u>

If we are to believe in the phrase 'an eye for an eye' then surely, neither party will have any eyes left at the end of a conflict.

Day 21

<u>Stirring it up - An analogy.</u>

We live our lives splashing around in the water, trying to see what's going on beneath the surface, whilst making it worse by stirring up the mud. If we stay still for a while, as within our minds, then the mud settles and things become much clearer to us.

Day 22

The big toe learning experience.

If you stub your big toe on the furniture, would your toe get angry with the furniture? No, of course not. Then why should we get angry with ourselves or others over mistakes? Acknowledge what happened, learn and move on.

Day 23

In everything I see, I see a piece of me.

We are all connected to the universe and each moment is unique to our own experience.

Day 24

<u>*Life is like a river.*</u>

We journey from a single spring to meet many others on the way, gaining momentum and breadth as we go, eventually meeting the great expanse of sea at the end of life's journey.

Day 25

<u>*Human Motor.*</u>

Our bodies are like motor cars. We need to give ourselves regular maintenance to avoid breaking down. It's best not to go too fast or we risk permanent damage.

Sometimes we need replacement parts to keep us going a bit longer. Eventually, we break down and get taken out of service.

Day 26

Disappearance in an Instant.

Why do we waste so much time and energy trying to solve problems within our minds through worrying? Break free from this imaginary world and the problem disappears instantly leaving you energised and in control again.

Day 27

Liberation from slave to master.

If somebody upsets you do you react with anger? Does the anger make you feel bad? Instead, pause for a while, still the mind and fill your heart with love and forgiveness. You will liberate your mind and find peace.

Day 28

Big is low and small is high.

Big things, like the oceans, would not exist if it weren't for the little things, like the streams, that spring from a higher source.

Day 29

Rome was not built in a day.

If you want to achieve something but are put off by the scale of it, try focusing on each stage, be patient, take one day at a time. The sum of the mini achievements will help you towards your goal.

Day 30

There's no 'I' in 'team'

As with a goal scorer in a game of football, an individual's performance is often as good as the people they work with. So, best not to praise or criticise an individual too much without considering the whole team.

Day 31

Time to wake up.

We live much of our lives in a dream state. Try to remember to wake up and see the world around you, as if for the first time. Add nothing...take nothing away.

Day 32

If Women Ruled The World.

Just about every war that ever was, started with the male of our species. So, to bring about world peace, only women should be appointed to rule.

Day 33

You are what you believe...you choose.

Whatever your mind believes, so it will be. Believe in negativity, create problems and misery, or; choose to be positive, create happiness and peace. Which will you choose right now?

Day 34

<u>Fooling your subconscious.</u>

What is our subconscious? Since it can't be seen, heard or touched how do we know it exists? Is it God, spirit or ego? They say it controls our emotions and intuition; that it automatically makes you feel negative without us knowing why. If so, why not reverse your fortunes and tell it how wonderful the world is and bring on a smile. If the subconscious is easily fooled either way, then far better to choose happy over sad.

Day 35

Charity begins at home.

If you want to solve the world's problems and help people, start with yourself.

Day 36

Subjective minds.

The same circumstances can affect different people in different ways. Is there a right or wrong? Take responsibility for your Self by looking inwards rather than outwards.

Day 37

Dirty minds think alike.

As with the dust that settles around the home, our minds get clouded without us noticing it. It is only when we clean the dust away that we are able to make a comparison and realise how dirty it was, leaving us to let the truth in.

Day 38

Over 100 billion...fancy that.

Physical and mental attributes were passed down from our parents (and the cosmos?) when we were born, then a multitude of influences shaped us from childhood to adulthood. Maybe 100 billion of us since we humans evolved and we're all unique.

Day 39

Switch it on and you will receive it.

As with a TV signal, just because love is invisible it does not mean that it is not there. You just need to switch it on to receive it.

Day 40

Fear of failure - Fear of freedom.

If you are ruled by fear of failure, then you shroud yourself with protective layers whereby nobody can see the real you. This conflict within yourself leads to unhappiness and yet you are conditioned to believe this is normal. Learn to let go and you will be free.

Day 41

I have confidence in me.

If you were a confident person, then you would no longer need to defend yourself.

Day 42

__Win - Win.__

Winning an argument can be like losing to the ego. True winning is cooperation.

Day 43

__Life is such a comedy.__

We're all trying to achieve the same goal...eternal happiness. It's just that we tend to take the scenic route and sometimes get lost on the way. We take our eyes off the road and lose the map. Life is such a comedy.

Day 44

Masters of the universe?

We can be masters of all kinds of things. Right the way from making a good meal to walking on the moon. We've done it all! But can we master ourselves?

Day 45

Escape from your own prison.

Don't worry about expressing yourself freely for fear of disapproval. You will create your own prison from which only you can escape.

Day 46

Mythical perfection.

Do not believe that life should be perfect, for perfection is a myth that we have created in our minds and will lead to disappointment.

Day 47

<u>Seek and you will find.</u>

The affects of the past have shaped our thoughts and feelings. If this has led to habitual unhappiness, it is possible to learn and develop new thoughts, and positive feelings. Seek and you will find.

Day 48

<u>Our every need fulfilled?</u>

Our modern world is full of gadgets that aim to fulfil our every need without having to make an effort or be creative.

If the real world is Creation itself then surely we are at odds with it.

Day 49

<u>Look ahead and miss the 'now'</u>

Best not to look too far ahead, lest you miss what's right under your nose.

Day 50

<u>It takes one to know one.</u>

Don't spend time judging others as you will attract that which you create.

Day 51

Recipe for life.

Recipe for a happy life: 4lb of regular fresh fruit and veg', 10 ounces of adequate sleep, 1 dozen of daily exercise, 3 tablespoons of reasonable working hours, 6 bunches of good relationships and optional sex. Bind together with an abundance of love and share.

Day 52

Motivational change.

Do we have to suffer adversity in order to become motivated enough to bring ourselves to enlightenment?

Day 53

Working together to keep harmony on-board.

Emotions are like the wind on a sail that propels you forward. Intellect is like the rudder of the boat that steers you in the right direction. It is better that these two work in harmony to keep you 'ship shape'.

Day 54

The answer is...there is no answer.

We can strive all our lives searching for the meaning of life, pondering over many things that are philosophically stimulating, without end. The answer is...there is no answer. There is only the present, what is now. We just need to wake up to this and go with whatever makes us happy.

Day 55

Four ways to be.

In silence, there is wisdom. In humility, there is peace. In letting go there is freedom. In forgiveness, there is love.

Day 56

The rocking horse of worry.

Worrying is like a rocking horse. It doesn't get you anywhere.

Day 57

Touching God.

When the mind reaches ultimate stillness, then you are touching God my friend.

Day 58

Giving strength to judgement.

To be judgmental is to give strength to that which should be avoided.

Day 59

Discipl-e to Discipl-ine

To be a disciple of Truth you have to be quite disciplined.

Day 60

Small steps make a stairway to heaven.

Many of you have been conditioned from an early age to feel guilt, which brings on a sense of low self-esteem. You then seek to make things better by relying on stimulants (alcohol, drugs, sex, caffeine, action movies etc.), which lasts only for a fleeting moment in time. Go back to the source and love yourself first. Unconditionally. It takes time but small steps make a whole stairway to heaven.

Day 61

<u>Respect the elderly.</u>

Respect the elderly for they have had more time on this earth to learn about life. One day you too will be elderly and will wish for the same respect and support.

Day 62

Taming the wild horse.

Meditation to quieten a busy mind is good in order to see more clearly. This might lead you to think that all thinking is bad and then get annoyed with yourself. Realise that thoughts are a part of your natural existence. We need to use our thoughts in order to live. Even if it is just to plan the next meal. The key is to observe our thoughts with self-compassion and understanding. We will then break in the 'wild horse' and become its master.

Day 63

Ask and you shall be given.

There are religious sayings such as 'Ask and you shall be given' and 'Seek and you shall find'. Surely, if this was true then we would have all won the lottery by now. No, I think this refers to peace of mind and happiness that we all seek ultimately, which is in reach of everybody.

Day 64

Open your heart and be thankful.

*Be thankful for every beating moment.
Be thankful for the senses we have.
Be thankful for the beautiful creatures in nature.
Be thankful for the splendid scenery on this earth.
Be thankful for the friends, relatives and acquaintances in our lives.
Be thankful for all the love this brings.*

Day 65

To be or not to be.

To be at peace with yourself requires the least effort. The minute you try to hold onto it, it disappears.

Day 66

High achievers are often insecure.

Only the insecure strive for security. Often you find this in the high achievers in life. So, high achievers are often insecure.

Day 67

Learning always solves depression.

Learning always solves depression. It helps focus the mind and diverts it from illusion to reality.

Day 68

Know Thyself.

Know thyself first and everything else will fall into place.

Day 69

Ode to Living.

As the years go on and on, my senses numb and yearn for rest.
As the days go hurtling by, my youthful fire sets in the west.
For as a child and all was new, I gathered grew and planted seeds.
Until I reaped my lasting ways, the fallen of forgotten needs.
B. Haines (1987)

Day 70

Life takes care of itself.

Life takes care of itself, despite our interference. So, when you get a bad feeling, let it float away as if it was the lightest thing on earth.

Day 71

Be master over you own house.

Be master over your own house, otherwise its servants will be mischievous. Be master over your own mind, lest your thoughts run riot.

Day 72

One day at a time.

Take life one day at a time. Do not think of tomorrow or yesterday, for they do not exist in the present.

Day 73

Being > Doing.

People should not consider so much what to do as much as what they are. The way to do is to be.

Day 74

The truth will set you free.

We must clear our minds to get a true picture of life. Even though we do not realise how much there is that stops the truth from being received. Have faith and the truth will set you free.

Day 75

Changes - This is the way of the world.

After pleasure, there is pain. After life, there is death. After excitement, there is stagnation. This is the way of the world. Let it flow like water from the mountains. Claim nothing for yourself for it always changes. We are all part of love and light.

Day 76

The difference between wanting and needing.

Your actions might be the same but the thought behind each are different. I might want to contact friends to socialise, or I might need to contact friends out of desperation. 'Want' is of free will, whilst 'need' is a necessity. So if you depend on something, you are no longer yourself, but are ruled by that thing.

Day 77

It was all in the mind.

Try to connect with the physical aspects of life. Whatever your problem is about, look at that problem with your senses, not your mind. See where that problem is and surely it will have disappeared. It was all in the mind after all.

Day 78

What we need to lubricate our journey through life.

Just as an engine needs oil to prevent it from overheating, we too need spiritual contact in order to lubricate our journey through life.

Day 79

Fight the good fight or give it up?

When people say 'don't give up' and 'fight the good fight', I say 'give up and find something easier that you enjoy doing'. There are a great many things in this world that can be enjoyed, not endured. Look inwards as well as outwards.

Day 80

Does God really exist?

If you doubt that God is real, then God must have existed at some point in the past for you to have known about 'Him'. Since God is eternal, 'He' must still exist today. Since God is omnipresent, there's no need to doubt any more. You just need to open your mind's eye and see 'Him' in everything.

Day 81

A lame state of affairs.

Just as a lamed body can't walk, a depressed mind can't think.

Day 82

We do not know the real world.

Our 5 senses pick up information about the world about us and sends that information to the brain. The brain then interprets this information based on its own physical method of processing colour, smell, touch etc., familiarity with the past, judgement (likes and dislikes). So, we do not know what the world about us is really like, only what our physical/mental attributes tell us.

Day 83

I have seen the light!.

I once took a picture directly at the sun using a mobile phone and when I checked the photo it showed a black silhouette of a flying saucer in the middle. People were convinced that there were extra-terrestrial beings at large. I later found out that this is an anomaly in the way the phone processes light and there was nothing strange about it at all. Similarly, our lives can be ruled by fear based on false perceptions. If we take away that false perception, we take away the fear too, and see the light as it truly is.

Day 84

What is the world for me now?

By saying this you help trigger an awakening response within you. You may realise at this point that you are not your body but you are the observer. You are living in the present.

Day 85

Daily exercise to find peace.

Sit comfortably. Empty the mind of any thoughts. Feel the whole body as you focus on your in-breath and relax on each outbreath. After a while open the senses to the sounds and sights around you. Then broaden the mind beyond your senses to feel your presence in the universe. Hold this for 5 or 10 minutes, all the while refocussing on the exercise whenever the mind wonders. Enjoy the peace within.

Day 86

Our built in Sat Nav.

Our feelings are like a sat nav that knows where we should be going. If we pay attention to what it is saying, it will guide us along our journey. If we ignore it then we may steer off-course and feel regret.

Day 87

In 10 year's time what will it matter?

If you feel bad, worried or concerned about anything, say to yourself, 'What will it matter in 10 years' time?'. Did anything that worried you 10 years ago help you find happiness today? Probably not...it just got in the way.

Day 88

We are one in a 7 billion.

About every quarter of a second around the world someone is born and possibly someone dies every half a second. With over 7 billion people alive at any one time it reminds me of how insignificant we are.

Day 89

Silent minds.

Let the mind become silent and the truth will come through on its own accord.

Day 90

News flash! Happiness has been discovered.

What is the one thing in life that you want the most? You might say more money, the latest T.V., a reliable car, a dream holiday or an ideal partner. Whatever you want, they all lead to your idea of happiness. Is it wise to rely on all these things that are beyond your control and do not last? Maybe if we look within ourselves, we might realise that happiness was there all along.

Day 91

See yourself in everything.

See yourself in everything. Love everything as you would love yourself.

Day 92

Why wait when you can live in heaven already.

Why wait to die before going to heaven when you can have it now and live in heaven on earth.

Day 93

The play of life.

Try not to attached yourself to your job and ambitions as if that's all you are. It is not life itself. We all have a role to play in life and so enjoy acting your part in the play of life.

Day 94

Helping others - Helping yourself.

Try to be helpful towards others, for in helping others, you are helping yourself.

Day 95

Welcome uncomfortable feelings as a friend.

Whatever feels negative or uncomfortable, either mentally or physically, give it your full attention and instead of fighting it, welcome it as a friend.

Day 96

Does time really exist?

Does time really exist? Only our memory of the past gives us a perception of passed time. Our imagination gives us our perception of the future. Both take place in the mind and thus we cannot see, touch or hear it, so is it real?

Day 97

Making a conscious effort at sea.

We can drift through life like a piece of wood being tossed around by the sea. Or we can wake up and make a conscious effort to realise our presence on the sea, take in the scenery and enjoy riding the waves.

Day 98

Let go the chains.

Let go the chains of the past. They will weigh you down and make you weary.

Day 99

Think big, think illusion.

I had a thought. Think of all the other people in this world right now who are thinking. What significance is my thought amongst many? How small and insignificant I am and yet how important I feel as an individual. Are thoughts real? If not, then the human race is living life in an illusion.

Day 100

Slow down your thinking.

Slow down your thinking. Ask yourself 'Who is this thinker', 'Who is it that sleeps, walks, talks, feels and thinks'. Feelings, emotions, hate, lust, likes, dislikes, passion, anger and body are not your true self. Once you take a step back from all this, you begin to find peace.

Day 101

It's a plant's life

A plant will respond to light, heat, water and earth, but will not bend a certain way or turn a certain colour when you wish it to. Life is like that. It will not behave, whether good or bad, to your wishes, because life was made like the plant...natural.

Day 102

Master of the house and keeping in order.

When a person makes you angry, you are more-or-less giving up control over your thoughts and feelings and letting someone else control them.
Why not be master of your house? If we put our own house in order, everything else will simply fall into place.

Day 103

Life is like a train journey.

Life is like a train journey. The faster you go the more thrilling it is. But your journey will draw to a close quicker and you will have missed everything on the way.

Day 104

A moment in infinity.

If I am part of the product of the past and part of the causes for the future, then I am situated in an infinite space of time. I am joined to all things and all things are joined to me in this space of matter and time. What lies beyond is too far a step for me to comprehend.

Day 105

My illusory prison.

Feeling down? Things aren't going your way? Annoyed at something? You will most likely blame everybody else and in doing so will never find peace within yourself. If you want to change all this, stop judging others, stop judging yourself, stop the blame for others and of yourself. Guilt is a made-up illusion that imprisons your mind. See this and you will realise that the prison that you made had the door open all the time for you to walk out and be free.

Day 106

Projection of the mind.

Whatever you project your future to be. So shall you become.

Day 107

Feel the expanse of our Universe.

If we break down every living creature, every inanimate object, every world, star and the space in-between, down to the minutest molecule we can see that we are all connected to the Universe and to one-another. Bring quietness to your mind for a moment, expand your consciousness and you might get a glimpse of it.

Day 108

<u>All bets on God to win.</u>

Not sure whether to believe in God? Not sure what God is? We live in a society where without hard evidence then God does not exist. On the other hand, millions of people and many cultures going back as far as history has recorded believe in a higher order of some sort. Mankind has proven many times over that there's more to our universe than we already know. So, why not take a leap of faith and go with God, love, peace and eternal life. Sounds like a good horse to back if I was a betting man.

Day 109

How not to become an alien.

Should we strive to get on well with all people? Perhaps by alienating ourselves from people we dislike, we are alienating ourselves from all people. If so, it is not for us to choose who we like or dislike, or to lay judgement on ourselves or others. Thus, we learn to keep an open mind regardless of who we have contact with in our lives.

Day 110

Why worry when you can care instead.

Somebody once said to me I need to worry more about my job. How could this be since I spent most of my time caring about it. Is there a difference? If I do not worry about my family does that mean I care less? I believe that worrying is something that goes on in the mind, it is fictitious, wears you down and is not in the present moment. Caring is what goes on in the real world through action and thoughtfulness. Worrying can actually stop you caring as you turn in on yourself as a kind of selfishness.

Day 111

Roll it up and throw it away.

Worrying about something? Gather these thoughts into a pile and imagine rolling them up into a ball. Throw the ball as far as you can into an imaginary lake. It's a very deep lake. There...gone. You should be able to see more clearly now and deal with situations more easily.

Day 112

Perfection in imperfection.

It can be quite frustrating striving for perfection and never achieving it. Why? ...because perfection does not exist. Sometimes it is worth giving yourself a break and be imperfect for a change. You might discover your true natural self as we were all created. Now that's perfection.

Day 113

<u>Births and Deaths</u>

They both seem to come and go in their own time. Often unexpected. Without the probability of one, you would not have the inevitability of the other. What is useful is that we accept both equally with a sense of both contentment, joy and adventure.

Day 114

Bend with the wind my friend.

We should live our lives like a blade of grass in the wind.
As the wind blows and things get difficult, we bend like the grass, and so adapt to new conditions with flexibility.
If we were rigid, like a dead bull rush, we would be fixed in our ideas and not able to bend with the wind. We would eventually break.
Therefore it is better to go with the flow and accept change, rather than hang on to the past that is no longer suitable to our changing world. Flowing this freely should bring joy.

Day 115

Joy or Fear = Life or Death.

Most of us have a fear of dying at least some times in our lives.
That deep dread of the unknown and

*possible pain as your body finally packs up.
What is one to do about
it? Nothing......you cannot avoid death no matter what you do.
So, can we avoid fear?. This is where we have the real choice in life. Whether you live in joy or in fear. The outcome will be the same.
So make the choice and live in joy.*

Day 116

Fight or Flight - Should I stay or should I go.

*With all the confrontation that we see in our daily lives is it better to fight or take flight?
To fight, you become the very thing that you are against, because you become more negative about everything and more confrontation will be attracted to you.
To flight seems to be a kind of avoidance*

as a result of fear. Issues within yourself well never be resolved if you run away as a result of fear.

The middle ground is to take a backward step, observe, be impartial, do not take sides, see how the play of minds can take over a person but do not be that person who is angry or in conflict. At this point you can choose where you want to be and who you want to be with. Go to people and places with a positive atmosphere and you will attract positivity into your life and feel nourished.

Day 117

<u>Live every day as if it were your last.</u>

Live every day as if it were your last. Could you bear to go out on your last day after losing your temper, with anger and worry in your heart?

Could you never have fully got to know you partner or children through years of being insular?

Would you regret having never said sorry for the things you said and did?
Would you wish you'd gone for one more walk in the woods, but this time really enjoy your surroundings?
So, live every day as if it were your last and you will awaken as if it was your first.

Day 118

Recipe for life

To live a full and happy life you need a mix of ingredients in the right proportions.
Recipe:
Regular exercise
Continuous learning
Creativity
Friends and acquaintances
Family relationships
Eat fruit and vegetables
Philosophical or religious beliefs
Good balance of work, rest and play
Time to relax, meditate and sleep
Put into the oven of life and cook for 100

*years or until done.
People that live long lives say 'everything in moderation'.*

Day 119

I am the observer.

Be the observer of your life. By being detached in this way, you are no longer affected by the troubles of the mind or day-to-day adversities. If you can do this, then inner happiness will follow.

Day 120

Be the master of your boat - Part I

*If someone is annoying you..., send them images of love.
If a situation becomes intolerable..., rise above it and look down on it.
If you are in pain to the point of tears..., be still for a while and focus the mind.*

Day 121

Be the master of your boat - Part II.

If you catch your mind falling into chaos..., use your five senses and bring yourself back to reality.
If your mind cannot decide what to do..., make it silent and let the heart decide.
If you fear someone of something..., do not dwell on it but be its friends.
Be the master of your boat and you will steer safely though life's changing seas.

Day 122

Wholly holy.

If prophets like Jesus or Muhammad lived the most holiest lives and yet were persecuted, what chance do we have against what would appear to be a sometimes cruel world. Maybe the lesson here is life is what it is, for better or for worse. It's how we deal with it, inside our minds, that counts.

Day 123

<u>The eternal moment in time.</u>

Whilst I am on the journey of enlightenment I will never reach my goal. So long as I keep travelling, I will never come to rest at the eternal moment in time.

Day 124

<u>The challenge of oneness.</u>

By being quiet, we are able to get in touch with ourselves.
When in touch with our higher selves, we feel the love in a moment's glory.
To feel the love, we pour out our heart and dispel our fears.

*Can we hold that way of being throughout each day?.
This must be the challenge of all life's challenges.*

Day 125

<u>*The knotted mind.*</u>

*A worried mind is like a knotted string. You might be tempted to pull it tighter hoping it will go away but you only pull the knot tighter and the worries get more stressful.
Let go of the knot. Take the pressure off it as you would a troubled mind. The knot will loosen; you will be able to see how to unravel it more clearly and the stress will go away.*

Day 126

The religion of celibacy and homosexuality.

Should religious leaders be celibate? Should they be allowed to practice homosexuality?

'Religion' is split over these issues and yet they proclaim to hold up universal beliefs. Centuries of dogma has masked the truth.

It's not the act that is important but what is within the mind. To live a truly religious life is to be free of judgement and guilt, or preconceived ideas about right and wrong. It is to live in an open, loving and forgiving manner that will bring the answer in accordance with natural laws, which is true religion.

Day 127

Reflections of your self.

*Be still in your mind.
As you would allow the surface of water to become still, with no ripples or waves. Then you will be able to see your own reflection more clearly on the surface. As you allow the mind to quieten in this way, you will see your self more clearly and there you will find peace and love.*

Day 128

Living in the heavenly moment.

Why wait to die before going to heaven when you can live in the moment and be there in an instant.

Day 129

Strong views = imprisoned mind.

Do you have any strong views or ideas about anything? If you are honest with

yourself, the chances are that it is making you unhappy. You may not even realise this but fixing the mind on anything can make you bonded to it, leading to an imprisoned mind.
Learn to let go and you will be free.

Day 130

Letting go of letting go.

Once you have learned to let go, you have to let go of the idea of letting go in order to truly let go.

Day 131

Working philosophy - Part I

Look after your workers and they will look after the work.

Day 132

Working Philosophy - Part II

Take your work seriously but do not take yourself seriously.

Day 133

Does fate exist, or are we rules by chaos?

*What determines our fate in life?
Is it all predetermined by a higher God like power, for which there is no choice?
Is it dependent on where and when we were born in relation to the planets and stars?
Does it depend on who our parents were and how we were conditioned from an early age?
Do we make our own choices and create our own futures?
Is the universe full of chaos, so although things seem predictable for a while,*

*ultimately everything is random?
I'm sure you agree that action=reaction and cause=effect.
So, maybe the answer is...they are all true.*

Day 134

What is God?

*I once heard on the radio that after much research, a conclusion was reached that there is no evidence that God exists. Interesting, because at the turn of the 19th century it was thought we had discovered everything there is to know.
It is worth considering God since most people would agree 'He' is personified as all-powerful.
So, without evidence, here's my believe: God is a man-made name for everything in the universe to infinity.
God includes everything we can sense and those realms that we humans are*

not capable of sensing.
So, it requires faith that there is a higher power. In scientific terms, it includes all those things that we have yet to discover, which could be one trillionth times what we know right now.
Maybe I have scratched the surface of truth, which opens the door to God.

Day 135

<u>Rules of life?...What rules?</u>

The only rule in life is that there are no rules.
Without rules you are not burdened or tied down.
Of course this assumes in the goodness of mankind.

Day 136

___The untrained mind is like a cork on the sea.___

An untrained mind is like a cork bobbing around on the sea. It has no direction, no control over its destiny and just gets blown about in all conditions.

Day 137

___Nine tips for amazing relationships___

1. Switch roles - imagine being the other person
2. Speak positively - pay compliments
3. Do not criticise - communicate with love
4. Forget ego and pride - be detached
5. Listen and understand - only speak when you have something to say
6. Do not speak from anger - verbal wounds may never heal
7. Winning an argument is like losing to the ego - true winning is cooperation

8. Let go of anger and self-righteousness - embrace love
9. Once the cause of anger is determined - let go instantly, not later.

Day 138

Fear of happiness - Part I

I, like most others, wish I was eternally happy. It's almost like a lifetime pursuit. What stops us from being happy? Well, the constant chatter within the mind, the hopes and fears, a resulting emotional roller coaster, but always not achieving happiness.
So, what are we thinking right now? A background dullness and sadness, even when not stressed.
If happiness can be achieved swiftly, simply by clearing the mind, disposing of all those hopes and fears, then why not do it?
RIGHT NOW!
It can work. It's a massive transformation.

Habit might eventually return us to our old ways so it needs daily practice of letting go.

Day 139

Fear of happiness - Part II

So, if the way to happiness is letting go, then how easy is it to let go?
It might seem like letting go is not caring. However, by letting go, you naturally care from within as a result.
The difference is that the chattering mind is not getting in the way.

Day 140

Life is like a mirror.

Whatever image you project out in life, it will reflect back to you. Good or bad, hate or love, despair or joy. Your choice.

Day 141

Antidote to fear, intolerance and anger

There is an underlying reason why we get intolerant and angry.
If we can catch the moment and understand why, then we might find it is built on fear and threat. For example, fear of being late or threatened by getting something wrong.
Instead of fighting back with more anger, why not pause and observe your thoughts for a second. See your actions and hear your words for what they are. Be detached, be simple, tolerant, considerate without illusion.
With practise, you will happily and successfully deal with anything that comes your way.

Day 142

No pain....Lots to gain.

*Some would say that we are put on this planet in order to advance ourselves.
Some would feel abandoned when they feel pain and suffering.
I believe there is no need for pain or suffering in our lives and we can all strive for this.
Adversity cannot be avoided but we can decide whether to be affected by it.
And so whether you feel pain or pleasure why not transcend all this and not let it control us.
We can then help each other, change the world and ultimately help yourself.*

Day 143

Time to wake up!

We dream when we sleep by living out a fantasy world that is a projection of our own mind.

*We dream when we are awake by living out a fantasy that the world is a playground for the ego.
So, what's the difference?
Must be time to wake up!*

Day 144

Problems and solutions are all one in an instant.

*Imagine that all your problems and grievances came from one source. So, whatever problems you encounter in life it's all down to one thing; how you feel inside, and not outside yourself after all. Imagine this one overarching problem had just one solution and that solution was not something you had to learn in time but attached to the problem in the same instant.
So whenever you encounter a problem, the solution will flip it over in an instant. You would realise straight away there was no problem after all.*

Life would be bliss. Aspire to this goal and you will achieve it.

Day 145

Happy to be growing older

*Maybe you feel depressed at the thought of getting older.
Think again. What's the alternative?
Be grateful for each day and rejoice in life.*

Day 146

Peeling back the layers of life.

*As we go through our lives we cover ourselves with layers, or influences that shape the way we are.
Layer upon layer we can no longer see the source and sometimes forget who we*

really are.
We can remove these layers and reveal the true self without fear or sadness but with love for self and all beings.
By removing these layers it will help us to see reality more clearly.

Day 147

<u>**Open your parachute and enjoy the ride.**</u>

Life is like a parachute jump.
We have the parachute to make sure our landing is nice and safe.
However, we forget to open it properly and end up getting tangled, and in a mess.
Like a parachute, we must open our hearts and minds to enjoy the ride and land safely.

Day 148

Outward Weakness / Inner Strength

In our culture, we often think that giving in to others is a sign of weakness.
For example, holding the door for someone to pass through and letting them go first.
Not so...the person who can go the extra mile in helping others with full-hearted, well-meaning is the person who has the inner strength.
The person who does not, in defending their actions, becomes weak and detached from reality.

Day 149

He who shouts loudest...

He who shouts loudest, gets his own way.
He who communicates saves the day.

Day 150

One of the greatest gifts given to mankind is choice.

We are free to roam the world, go to the moon, stop world poverty, make ourselves extinct and build machines to do every task.
How we use this gift, for good or for evil, is our choice.
When we become blind to this gift we become motivated by greed, fear and hatred, which masks the truth of who we are and thus continue to make the wrong choices.

Day 151

The everlasting journey - Part 1

Apparently, the life we have is just one of many that we have chosen for ourselves, during our time in heaven when our spirit decides what lesson we wish to learn on earth.

*Thus, the soul is on an endless journey, without beginning or end.
So, it's no good thinking everything will be alright when we go to heaven. We have to create heaven on earth right now, in every minute of our lives.*

Day 152

<u>The everlasting journey - Part 2</u>

*If you ever doubt the existence of this everlasting journey, consider the proof that exists.
Look at the starts. Do you see the end of the universe? No, it goes to infinity.
Look at your hand. Do you see the smallest particle? No, it goes on to be ever-smaller.
Consider time. Does it stop at some point? No, it goes on for ever.
As part of the cosmos...this is the proof that we are eternal.*

Day 153

Young person Old person. There's no difference.

What's the difference between a young person and an old person? Answer...nothing. What separates the two is time. Since time is an illusion of the mind's memories, then there is no difference.

Day 154

The door of our cage has always been open.

Metaphorically, we live in a tiny cage where there is no peace of mind because we feel trapped and undernourished. We do not realise that the cage door is not locked and that we are free to escape any time we like. How pointless our lives have been when we realise that we can walk free anytime, into the light.

Day 155

Dying in the future or living in the present?

Why worry about whether there is life after death, when it's not important. Everything changes anyway so why not go with it. Once you have learnt to let go of ideas of the future you will be left with what life is for you now. Living in the present is a far better option if you want to find true happiness.

Day 156

It's easy to worry about everything...

It's easy to worry about everything but harder not to worry about anything.

Day 157

The world is a beautiful place.

*Go out into the fresh air.
Go for a walk in the woods, through parks and fields.
Climb a hill or mountain and see the spectacular views.
This small part of the world is but a sample of the beauty to behold.
The oceans and seas, the mountains and valleys, the vast expanse of flat land , rivers and cloud formations, ever changing with the weather.
The huge array of animals, birds, insects, fish and unimaginable creatures that roam the planet.
We are indeed in a very special place, sandwiched between ground, sea and sky. Part of the universe.*

Connected.

Day 158

The spirit is thicker than water.

*There's a saying that blood is thicker than water, which means families stick together more than friends and acquaintances.
It is also said that the spirit is thicker still. Thus, all beings (us) stick together more than any individual relation.*

Day 159

Love...to the exclusion of all others?

*Christian marriage vows ask couples to be joined together, to the exclusion of all others.
So, does this mean the Church does not allow universal love once you are married?
Oops.*

Day 160

Tidy House - Tidy Mind

The mind is like your house; if you keep it in good order then it functions much better.

A messy house has too many obstacles and discomforts to be able to function easily. Just as with your mind, if it holds too much clutter (thinking too much and worrying) it loses clarity.

And so, just as a daily routine of tidying up gives you a better quality of life, so does a daily helping of meditation and clearing the mind, gives a more composed, controlled way of thinking.

Day 161

Life is a journey.

Life is a journey...not only through space and time but also a journey of the Self. Focus on being the driver of your vehicle and you will travel through life with much peace and confidence.

Day 162

The oneness of truth.

There are a thousand words of wisdom that can be said in all manner of ways and yet there is but one meaning. The oneness of truth.

Day 163

Like lambs...we think the grass is greener on the other side, despite the danger.

I once walked the hills around my local Snowdonia and came across 3 lambs in a very deep trench. Two were dead and another just stared at me not knowing what to do. I knew that it would be pointless trying to rescue the lamb because it would run away. I imagine the surviving lamb would have also died eventually.

Later I discovered another lamb with it's head stuck in a wire fence, gasping for air. I was able to free this one but each time I drew it from the brambles it took fright and kept lunging its head back in the fence.

Maybe we humans are like the lambs. Maybe we want to be helped but do not realise it and when help is offered we do not recognise it. And so, we are also lost.

Day 164

<u>The returning lamb.</u>

A stray lamb that has returned to the flock is like the straying mind that has come home to the truth.

Day 165

Fear of letting go - fear of flying.

*Have you ever had a relationship where it has been just as painful to leave that person as it has been to stay together?
A troubled life through habitual worrying is a bit like this.
If you let go of worrying it might seem as though you are left with nothing. The worrying at least fills a perceived gap or void.
This is where faith comes in. A leap of faith. Jump from your height of worry and you will see that you will be able to fly.*

Day 166

To have or to be.

*We can read a lot of books in pursuit of the path to perfection.
We can also attend classes in search for enlightenment.
At some point we have to put down our*

*books and stop listening.
At some point we need to reach the journey's end.
No more having - Time to start being.
The time is always now.*

Day 167

Brainy thought - One thing we do know is that we do not know.

*Experts say that a large proportion of the human brain can be cut out before it affects normal functioning. Also, that most of the brain is not used.
And yet, according to evolutionary theory, everything has evolved for a purpose.
So, does this mean that the unused part of the brain has evolved for another purpose? Maybe a purpose that we used to have but have no more. Or is it waiting for us to tap into it for some future*

purpose?
One thing we do know is that we do not know.

Day 168

<u>Are humans that foolish to think that we know what we are doing?</u>

We humans pride ourselves on all manner of achievements and yet some of the greatest discoveries were made by accident.

Day 169

<u>How to solve the world's problems.</u>

The world is a manifestation of what is in our minds and continues to manifest from our ideas, thoughts and feelings. Discrimination, love, war, peace, famine, abundance, pollution, clean environment...etc. So, if you want to solve the world's problems...start with your Self and put your mind in order, show love and be joyful and it will manifest itself.

Day 170

There are none so blind as we that can see.

Just as a blind person learns to interpret the world within their limited abilities, we too are unable to see the truth of the real world in which we live.
Instead we create our own version of what we think is reality. We then cling to it and fear losing it by defending it, not realisng our perception is just an illusion.

Day 171

The illusion of playing God.

We think that we have no control over our lives and yet if we look around us, we

*see all the many things that we have created.
We think that we created ourselves and yet choose to ignore the higher powers of creation that made all things.
No wonder we humans get so confused.
We have forgotten who we are.*

Day 172

<u>Who am I?.......I Am.</u>

*Ask yourself...'Who Am I?'
If you listen quietly you might come up with the answer...'I Am'*

Day 173

<u>Meditation...the art of quietening the mind.</u>

Meditation. This is hard to do if you have lived your whole life with a busy mind. Old habits die hard. Like a wild bull, it needs taming, through gentle coaxing. Even for a few moments, try focusing your breath. The air passing through your nose or mouth. Feel the gentle ebb and flow of your chest rise and fall like the ocean waves.

Keep your mind clear and enjoy the relaxation.

Day 174

The power of belief - Part 1

I've read that the desert rose (a stone made from sand), promotes clear thinking. So, I held one that I bought from a market in Tunisia, to my forehead. What do you know, it felt as though it was working!

Where's the science in this thinking? Can some stones harm you like eating some plants can?

Maybe belief is the power within itself. It would be foolish to assume that we know everything there is to know, as some late-

Victorians did. Maybe not, as a Reiki Master once told me that the healing will work even if you do not believe.

Day 175

The power of belief - Part 2

Believing in something casts doubt over its existence. There's no need to believe in something if you know it to be true.

Day 176

An attitude for gratitude.

Find a moment for gratitude and in that moment of humility when all things come to rest, far from the maddening crowd, you will find your home, your true Self.

Day 177

The illusion of being the best.

*Careful not to strive for perfection, lest you become imperfect in doing so.
Careful not to always want to be the winner, lest you lose friendship in doing so.
Careful not to become a master of everything, lest you become an expert of nothing.
Careful not to enrich yourself with worldly goods, lest you drain the world of all it's beauty.*

Day 178

You live by the sword, you die by the sword.

*Have you ever compared yourself to others, or others between themselves?
It's not the fact that people are different that causes problems, it's more about what you do with that information.*

*So, if you pass judgement on a person for their looks, where they live, what job they have, how much they earn...etc, you bring a negative aspect into your mind such as a feeling of superiority.
Because this feeling is at odds with reality, it causes you distress and you become more judgmental in order to justify yourself.
In turn this makes you more negative as you think one person is worth more or less than another. You reflect the very thing that you have made in your mind and thus believe you are worth more or less than another.
Hence the meaning of the saying, you live by the sword, you die by the sword.*

Day 179

More Mind Matters - Exercising the brain.

*Just like the body, the brain needs regular exercise in order to keep fit.
Reading a long book might be like*

*running a marathon.
Doing arithmetic might be like circuit training.
Working out how to fix something might be like playing football.
And, as with the body, you must remember to take a break after a while in case you burn out with mental fatigue.*

Day 180

Find your haven and be in heaven.

I guess it's no coincidence that haven, meaning safe refuge, is similar to heaven, paradise of the spirit world.

Day 181

What is Father and Son?

If you are struggling with the term 'Father and Son' within the Christian faith then here's a little guidance.

*Of course we all have a paternal father otherwise we would not have been born, and for that reason we are all sons.
Similarly, all of mankind was created from some source, depending on your beliefs. Scientifically, let's call it universal energy. You might also call it God.
And so this universal energy is our father and we are all sons of it.*

Day 182

<u>Love or disillusionment...you choose.</u>

*There are only two things that really matter in this world.... Love and Freedom of choice.
Every moment of your day you have the freedom to choose whether to live your life in love or move away from it towards disillusionment.*

Day 183

Where there's a Will there's a way.

You can help take control of your life by meditating. Just take a few moments out of your day and check in with your thoughts, body, emotions and surroundings.
Whatever you decide, it is always your Will that provides the motivation to do anything. The Will can steer you into living mindfully or mindlessly.
Choose wisely by friend.

Day 184

Whatever you seek in life, you will find.

Experts would say that an unhappy childhood can lead to an unhappy adult life. Sometimes leading to depression and even worse; self-harm such as drug and alcohol misuse.
The opposite might apply to those that come from a happy childhood. Happy

memories leave us with a positive outlook on life.
For those that have turned to self-harm or have low self-confidence, go out and seek people in life that can offer you love and compassion. This is what you are missing.
Whether it be self-harm or compassion, whatever you seek in life you will find.

Day 185

Spiritual mambo jumbo or a source of learning?

It's not so important to understand how spirituality works but more so, what you do with it.
You might be sceptical and not believe in some of that medium 'mambo jumbo'. That's fine, clear those judgements away, listen to what is being said and decide for yourself if it is useful regardless of its source.

Day 186

The interplay of consciousness(A) and subconsciousness(B).

Here's a formula for the interplay of consciousness(A) and subconsciousness(B):

Happy A feeds happy B = Feeling happy.
Happy A feeds miserable B = Living in the past.
Unhappy A feeds depressed B = Self defeatism.
Unhappy A feeds happy B = Meeting the challenge.
Note, the only true formula is the first, where both A and B are one. There's no dualism at all.

Day 187

Who Am I...brain or soul?

*We acknowledge our existence because our consciousness is aware of this. In otherwords, 'I am', therefore I exist.
So, what is consciousness?
Is it the function of the brain to be aware, without which, we would cease to exist?
So, what is the brain?
Is it a collection of billions of neurons (brain cells), working together to form the way we perceive and react to the world about us, including inventing fantasies within the brain?
So is that it? Our thoughts are merely physical or chemical interactions?
What of the soul?*

Day 188

<u>Press the pause button...all becomes still and calm.</u>

Our minds can be like a personal MP3 player, playing back different thoughts over and over again in our minds, at

different speeds and often multi-layered. We try to slow this down with alcohol or other forms of escapism but it just keeps coming back worse the next day, which just adds to the mind's confusion.
So what is there to do?
Press the pause button for a few moments. Enjoy the quiet. If the button is faulty, bring your mind back to rest by focusing your finger on the button.
If this is difficult, release the button and play words of your choosing, like "I am a likable person", " The world is a wonderful place" and "The universal presence all around me is my friend".
Press hold...and all becomes still and calm.

Day 189

Religious or not-religious, that is the question.

There are many religious faiths in this world. Some might say, filled with

*dogmas and misinterpretations.
One has to ask, is true religion about control, defence and damning all non-followers?
Or, is it about choice, truth and love?
Only the heart doth know.*

Day 190

We are all builders of the same bridge to heaven.

*There are many paths to truth and wisdom. All of them valid; all similar in their underlying message.
Do not force others to follow your path lest you lose your own. Respect each and every one. We are all builders of the same bridge to heaven.*

Day 191

Pickled lifestyles...

We appear to have got ourselves into a bit of a pickle when it comes to healthy lifestyle.

Many of us live unhealthy lives, leading to health issues, which are remedied through prescribed medicines. This then allows us to go on living unhealthy lifestyles and the circle continues.

Of those that stand to gain include the fast food chains, television and drug companies.

Maybe it's time to start asking ourselves, 'are we been misled?'.

Day 192

Newsflash!...recent discovery into 'Who am I?'.

Have you ever asked yourself, 'Who am I?'.

This implies there is both a questioner and a person who would provide the answer. No wonder it can't be answered! It also implies there are two people in the dialogue and therefore we are confused because in truth there is only one of us. In truth, 'I am my Self'.

Day 193

Let your body do its thing.

Most of us believe our minds and bodies are part of the same entity. So, when I am in pain I feel miserable and if I am depressed my body can get sick more often.

Instead, try this and see if you feel any healing...

Say to yourself, 'I am not my body', 'my body is a vehicle that I am occupying for a while', 'the body is very resilient and knows how to stay healthy without my interference', 'I will keep a healthy loving mind'.

Day 194

Nothing that we perceive in our world is real.

*Our biased view of life has been shaped by all that has gone before is.
What one person perceives is different to another because we all have different backgrounds, influences and make-ups.
I might say something is bitter and another say it was sweet. I might say it is cold and another would feel warm. I might hate someone that others adore.
There can only be one reality or truth in everything but we seem to be incapable of witnessing this.
This would imply that nothing we perceive in our world is real.*

Day 195

Sanity scale - Humanity scale.

Sanity.

How can we tell if the human race is not insane if we live in such a mad world with so much propaganda, violence, fear and poverty?

It is my belief that we are all insane; some more than others. We are all on a sliding scale of say 1 to 10 so that a 1 might be the wisest off all, whilst a 10 might be those that are locked up to protect themselves and others.

We might even move up and down that scale as we change our lives.

Embrace it and try to aim for a 1, but remember as brothers, we are all part of the same humanity scale.

Day 196

Waves of love and understanding.

Out of stillness comes a great wave of love and understanding.
You may not be expecting it but you

need to recognise it when it happens. Bask in it, enjoy it, for eventually the wave will recede.
There's always another.

Day 197

Peeling back the layers of perception.

There's no such thing as good or bad; just truth or illusion.

Day 198

The boatman and the millionaire.

There was a boatman who lived in the most beautiful seaside resort you could imagine. He made his living from giving private boat tours. He wasn't rich but was happy.

One day, a millionaire booked a tour and on the way, said to the boatman, "You should buy two more boats and grow the

business".
The boatman said, "Why should I do that?"
Millionaire, "So you can invest the profits into having more tour locations"
The boatman said, "Why would I want to do that?"
Millionaire, " So you can invest and grow into more countries"
Boatman, " Why would I want to do that?"
Millionaire, "So you can retire and live in the most beautiful seaside resort and be happy".
You see, we can drag our ambitions through the mill, only to find that that the ultimate goal is already with us.

Day 199

<u>Look under your nose to see beyond your horizons.</u>

In order to see what is beyond our horizons we have to first look at what is under our noses.

Day 200

<u>Insignificant me = Insignificant problems</u>

Imagine for a moment that you can see the horizon all around you.
The move your attention beyond the horizon to be aware of the entire country, all those fields, mountains, towns and cities.
Now expand your imagination to feel your tiny presence resting on the entire earth.
Go beyond earth, expanding your attention to be aware of space far beyond anything invisible to the human eye.
Realise how small you are; how microscopic you are like an atom in a vast universe that goes on for ever. Small

*and insignificant.
Does this not make you feel quite humble in a way that all your problems also seem small and insignificant?*

Day 201

Mirror, mirror on the wall, who is the best illusion of them all.

*Never compare yourself to others.
In our world of comparing there will always be someone better than yourself.
Thus, to criticise someone, to judge them or to belittle them is to criticise, judge or belittle yourself.
Like a mirror, it reflects the illusion back at you.*

Day 202

Why live the dream when you can live.

Every dreamt of a better life only to find that you never manage to achieve it. If head towards your horizons, like the end of a rainbow, you will never get there. Perpetual discontent follows. When we achieve our dream, we often find that it was not all that it was cooked up to be anyway and find it difficult to break the habit of dreaming of an even better life.
So, stop dreaming, wake up and live life.

Day 203

<u>Stay calm for greater clarity.</u>

Ever looked across a lake and admired the beauty of the scenery reflecting off the water?
Maybe life is like one big reflection. After all we rely on our senses to relay a picture of the real world to our brain. Sometimes making waves will distort what we see. As with the reflection of the lake, even

though we know it is only a reflection, we can still appreciate the beauty of what we see.
The calmer we are, the greater the clarity.

Day 204

Be master of your own house.

I once read that anger is good for you as it helps you vent your emotions rather than bottling it up leading to anxiety.
I am also led to believe that by being angry you are negatively affecting others, giving a domino effect in making the world a worse place.
So which is it to be....let it out or bottle it up?
What about the third way. Try a more passive, meditative style of thinking, pause for a moment and take control of your emotions. Be master of your house.

Day 205

Surfing the mindfulness wave.

Being calm in mindfulness is like riding the crest of a wave.
You have to focus to stay and you glide effortlessly through life.
Sometimes the waves come crashing in on you and you lose balance.
That's ok...just wait for the next wave, get on board and enjoy the moment.

Day 206

Strong on the outside - Fragile on the inside.

Ever known a bossy person, who is boisterous, blaming, impatient and belittling of others?
These people are often leaders as we would rather let them get their own way than challenge them and create conflict.

If you ask why this person is like this and dig under the surface, you will find that they are more insecure than you are.
If they get rid of their fear of failure then there would be no need for conflict. If they were more confident inwardly, there would be no need to mask their insecurity.
To recognise this in others is to recognise this in ourselves. So makes friends - we are one.

Day 207

**If all the world's a stage, then what play are you in?**

If all the world's a stage, then what type of play are you in?
A comedy, farce, tragedy or a love story?

Day 208

Living in a material universe.

Everything in the universe is made up of tiny matter, assembled in a way that we are able to identify it, label it and form an opinion of it.
But what of the mind's consciousness? The observer. Where is that?

Day 209

Rejoice...for we are One with the Universe.

We are one with the Universe. No one can deny we have superiority over all creatures. The world is a wonderful place. Open your hearts and minds, and rejoice.

Day 210

The journey from a maddening world to enlightenment.

Do you often think that it's a battle to keep your sanity above the maddening world around you?
Here's another way of looking at it:
We're all on a journey to find happiness. Most of our paths lead us to a dead end and we have to go back and try a different path.
Forget the material world, it may offer you fun for a while but eventually you will need to seek the one true path that leads to truth, freedom and joy.
Think that you have found this path and take a step back. Leave it to God to guide you. It's not your job to lead. Leave it to the expert.
Soon you will realise that behind you is all the maddening world made up of the mind's illusions. Leave it behind and keep walking on, on the one true path to enlightenment.

Day 211

Observe the mind.

*To constantly observe what is going on in our minds is to understand our minds much better.
It will lead to change and peacefulness.*

Day 212

The observer and the observed.

The observer and the observed are one and the same.

Day 213

All things in moderation.

I have often wondered if hiving yourself away from the rest of the world for long periods to meditate actually helps you to achieve anything.

*They say carrots are good for you but eating too many becomes toxic.
You learn how to have a quiet mind when you are on your own I guess
But, do you learn anything about life, friendship, sharing, caring or compassion.
If you have not lived life's experiences how can you learn anything?.
As they say, all things in moderation.*

Day 214

<u>Keeping your mind's house safe from harm.</u>

*If you were the master of your own house you would not let anyone in that would do you harm.
So why do you let in all those worries, fears, hates and judgments into your mind? They serve you no good.*

Day 215

<u>A day in the life of an unruly ego.</u>

We can help to live our lives more peacefully by disassociating ourselves from our egos.
After spending a life time of being whatever our ego dictates this is not easy.
The ego can be wild, unruly; make you feel sad and anxious, whilst looking for a way out through short lived pleasures.
It takes some practise, but if we disassociate ourselves from our egos by observing it from outside ourselves, then we begin to feel some relief.
Instead we can begin to quiet our egos, not being a slave to it any more, and allow the silence of truth to come flooding into our minds, our Selves.

Day 216

<u>Simply open the curtains of your life and the darkness will cease to exist.</u>

*If you feel that your life is full of darkness, which leaves you scrambling around in the dark not knowing which direction to turn.
If you live in fear because in the darkness you think that something is lurking in the shadows waiting to pounce on you.
If in the darkness you start to go insane as you try to make sense of your surroundings by making up false images.
Then simply open the curtains. Let go of the past. Let the light come flooding in and see the truth.*

Day 217

<u>**Things aren't always what they seem.**</u>

*As I look up into the night sky, I notice stars rising above the horizon.
Wait a minute, the stars don't move that quickly, it's the earth's rotation.
As I look up into the night sky, I notice two lights colliding with each other.*

Wait a minute, one's a plane and the other's a star, 10 million light years away. Since things aren't always what they seem, what else is out there that we think we understand but in reality, we know nothing at all.

Day 218

A poem for life - A poem for living.

*If all your life feels in disarray,
Take a few moments to pause the record play.
Take time out and listen to your voice,
Please remember that it's always your choice.
The blame and the hate, the judgement and fear,
Will all fall away when things become clear.
Go to the things that you enjoy best,
Never give up on this wonderful quest.*

Day 219

Who do we blame? Nobody of course.

When something bad happens, like an earthquake, people say that God does not care, or, he is punishing those who will suffer.

The problem with this thinking is that things happen as a natural function of the world we live in. An earthquake or a flood does not care where you live when it opens up.

A tsunami won't go around you because you asked it nicely.

Similarly, mostly everything you see around you is made by mankind. God did not make this, we did. And so we have to take full responsibility for our actions.

Blaming God is therefore mankind's way of continuing to behave badly with impunity.

Day 220

In forgiving other people you are actually lightening your burden and forgiving yourself.

We all know what forgiveness is and yet when we reflect on the person that has done us harm, forgiveness seems to be the hardest thing to do.
It seems simple but for some reason we struggle to let go of our grievances.
We have nothing to lose by forgiving. Try it, but do it willingly with feeling for the perpetrator.
It will take away the burden of hate that you carry so that in giving forgiveness, you are actually forgiving yourself, also healing yourself.

Day 221

What is the opposite of life?

*What is the opposite of life?
Death I hear you say.
Wrong !
Those that know eternal life know also that life has no opposites and death is but an illusion of the mind.*

Day 222

<u>Darkness is an illusion caused by the lack of light</u>

*If you feel worried, down or depressed it sometimes seems like an eternity.
An eternity of stirring into the darkness where you do not know how big it is or what is lurking around that might give you fear.
Just as you would shine a light in the darkness, you should mentally throw some attention onto the dark thoughts*

*and light them up.
By seeing more clearly the darkness disappears, like an illusion, you will no longer fear what is around you.*

Day 223

Thoughts that magically disappear in a puff of smoke.

*We have lazy minds. Allowing our thoughts to run away with us, constantly chattering in circles. It's a habit hard to break.
Take back control. Say 'From this day forth, I'm going to wake up, take back control and be my true myself"
Don't be separate to your thoughts as if they are not your own but be your thoughts whether good or bad. They will disappear in a puff of smoke.
By resting on this for a moment, engagement will follow and you will no longer be subject to all those ramblings that cloud your perception.*

Day 224

The greatest thing is the least likely to cause you harm.

What are you most likely to stumble over, a rock or a mountain?.
A rock of course.
Surely then, the greatest thing is the least likely to cause you harm.
What could be greater than peace and happiness.

Day 225

Intent....What will you choose?

Intent !
Perhaps one of the most powerful words there is.
With intent you can achieve anything.
With intent you choose which way you

wish to live.
Think about it now. What will you choose?

Day 226

Lay down you shield and realise, there's nothing to defend.

In our society, we are indoctrinated to believe that strength lies in aggression and in uncompromising ways.
Some people get their own way not because they are wise but because they breed fear, are intimidating and become uncompromising.
Well, I've got news for you!.
All these traits are the sign of a weak person because they do not know how to love and forgive. They are trapped in their own fear. Afraid of opening themselves up in case they are verbally wounded when their shield is down.
A truly strong person can open up and take everything on without fear or threat. By letting down your defence you realise

there was nothing to defend in the first place, only imaginary thoughts from a waking dream.

Day 227

<u>Building Your Recovery Capital</u>

Is it possible to take on anything that life throws at you and still remain peaceful, happy and at one with yourself? Sounds like a good theory. Try it and see how long you can last.
I suspect you would forget to be invincible but with practice you can build up your inner sanctity and stay on top for longer periods.

Day 228

<u>Over the hill?....Get over it!</u>

Some might say that once you've peaked it's downhill all the way.

Why not enjoy the free ride, you've earned it.

Day 229

Using our Recovery Compass

*Go inside yourself and listen to your inner voice every moment of the day.
It will say, I enjoy that, or, I do not like that.
Are you listening? Do you hear it but then ignore it?
We often do what is expected of us, go where the money is or feel obliged to commit to something thinking that deprivation is righteousness.
Surely, to ignore it is to bring on unhappiness To ignore your recovery compass is to steer your ship into the rocks of misery.
To go with everything your inner compass dictates must bring on the seas of mastery.*

Day 230

<u>Fore - giving: Up front - freely transferring</u>

*Harbouring grievances within yourself will eat at you until there's very little left.
And yet you can't let go because you feel you are right and that must be upheld.
What's the point if you just grow old and die a grumpy old slave to this illusion?
Or
Emitting forgiveness from within will make you creative and expend your horizons.
It teaches you to let go of your opinions about right and wrong.
This is the whole point of life, of freedom, of reality.
It starts with forgiving yourself.*

Day 231

See yourself shining back in someone else's shoes.

We are so quick to criticise that we rarely realise the impact it has on our wellbeing. Have you ever felt really happy after having criticised someone or something? Probably not. Why?
Because it makes you feel negative. Could be a form of self-guilt in their somewhere too.
Most errors that occur in other people, we recognise in ourselves because at some point in our lives we would have done a similar error.
So to judge others is to judge yourself and that makes us feel bad.
Put yourself in the other person's shoes and see yourself reflecting back through the shine.

Day 232

Living life to the full in Mindfulness

Meditation is not just for sitting still in a quiet room for hours.
Yes, this can be quite beneficial for a short while.
Meditation is for going out and living your life to the fullest, whilst still retaining a calm mind.
Being in control, every moment of each waking hour, living in the Now.
Some people call it Mindfulness.

Day 233

To compare is to confine yourself to a rigid set of delusional rules

Ever compared yourself to another?
Yes, of course we all have.
He's wealthier, she's more beautiful, they seem much more happier than me etc.
What about those who are worse off?
We dismiss those as unimportant.
And yet there's a lesson to be learnt here.
With over 7 billion people on the planet

*there's always going to be someone better off than you. There's always going to be someone worse off than you.
So why carry out this delusion of comparing or judging. It only makes you unhappy.
See the reality, be humble and you will be set free.*

Day 234

<u>An ode to the book of life</u>

*Life is like reading a book.
Every now and then you come to an end of a chapter,
Then start to read again from the beginning of the next.
Sometimes it gets so absorbing you can't put it down.
Other times it will get you so perplexed.
As you start to draw towards the end,
You're hoping there'll be an annex.
And when the final page is turned.*

All of life's quandaries will merely become text.

Day 235

Not a murderer, not a liar, not a thief, not pretentious....

Judge a man not by what he is, but by what he is not.

Day 236

All for one and one for all.

Does the sea know its name as the sea?
Does the land know its name as the land?
Does a tree know that it is called a tree?
Does the dessert know it is called sand?
These are all words that we humans have made up to make our journey through life more amenable.
We make each item individual and

separable
If we lift the veil that we cast over all that we see
We get a glimpse of reality.
All is one.

Day 237

An inner challenge of observation.

STOP!
Right now, and awaken.
Clear you head and feel the presence of your whole body from top to bottom.
Observe your breathing. Through your nose, mouth or chest.
Listen to the sounds around the room and to the furthest distance.
Look around the room and focus on different objects as if for the first time
Do not think or judge. Just observe.
Open all the senses to the whole wide universe. Go beyond the senses.
Surely this peaceful inner world is our natural state.

*Now for the real challenge...
Remain in this peaceful natural state for the rest of the day.*

Day 238

<u>Where do you want to live? In a cage or out to freedom?</u>

*There is a dog near to where I live, that lives in a cage most of its life.
It seems healthy, but howls and barks whenever there are people nearby.
I am surprised that when the owner lets it out, how content it is to go back in the cage after just half hour of freedom.
Are we also like that?
We seem to live most of our lives in a cage that we have created ourselves within our minds. Limited by self-imposed rules, judgements and fear of going beyond what we think people should perceive of us.
When we come out of the cage and get a glimpse of a whole universe of*

freedom, we do not know what to do. It seems so alien because it does not conform to the way we have been conditioned all out lives.
Only we can decide for ourselves if we prefer to live in a cage or venture out and experience freedom of mind.
Which do you think is our true selves?

Day 239

8.7 million species on the planet and we are the only ones that need money.

We say to ourselves, 'We need money to live'
It seems to go without saying because that's all we have known.
There are arguably 8.7 million species on the planet and out of all those species we are the only ones that need money to live.
Don't you find that a bit odd?
Are we not living a life of folly?

Maybe it's time we got back to nature and learn how to live.

Day 240

Secret to looking beautiful is revealed.

Some might spend a fortune on makeup, anti-wrinkle cream or even plastic surgery. All this to look beautiful.
And yet there is a free and simple way of achieving beauty far beyond anything you can put into words.
I am prepared to share my secret with you if you promise to share it with others.
Here it is...
A SMILE !

Day 241

Modern life is like a dogs tail. Always chasing it.

Ever seen a dog chase it's tail?
With much amusement the dog does not seem to realise that it is part of his body and the more he chases it, the more it gets away.
How much our modern life is like a dog's tail
Chasing our dreams only to find there's another one just ahead.
More of a sorrowful tale me thinks.

Day 242

The jailer and the jailed are one and the same.

Our thoughts of guilt, sorrow and fear can often make us feel imprisoned.
Our thoughts of judgement, comparing and importance above others can turn us into a prison keeper.
Either way, both are confined to the prison, whichever side of the imaginary bars you live.

The jailer and the jailed are one and the same.

Day 243

<u>If you break free from your prison, it will disappear.</u>

Jailer or jailed, it does not matter which world you live.
Both are the same.
Once you have broken free,
You will realise it was never there at all.

Day 244

<u>Today is the first day of the rest of your life.</u>

Stuck in the past?
Don't be.
Today is the first day of the rest of your life.

Day 245

The four levels of forgiveness:

I'm right, you're wrong = I'm trapped, you're worthless.

I'm right, I forgive you = I'm still trapped, you're less equal than me

I forgive myself, I forgive you = I'm free, we are all equal

There was nothing to forgive in the first place.

Day 246

Surprise gift for us all.

*We are all gifted in different ways.
As with any gift, we just need to know
how to take the wrapping off.*

Day 247

True vision without the need for eyes.

*True vision does not need a pair of eyes
True vision will shine through from the wise
True vision is within your heart and mind
True vision is given even if you're blind*

Day 248

The multi-tasking minds of men and women.

*Men may get a hard time from women
who say they can't multi-task.
Surely to focus the mind on one task at a
time is admirable. It will ensure your mind
is not split, leading to chaos and*

confusion.
To focus is to remain steady as a rock, unmoved, in control and enduring.
So, let us celebrate, to all those men and women who choose not to multi-task.

Day 249

The law of attraction. An attitude for gratitude.

Have you ever noticed, people that complain a lot always seem to live out their lives with something that goes wrong for them.
Also, that positive thinking people always seem to do the right thing and it goes right for them.
Some would say that there are universal force at work here in which you receive whatever you ask.
So, why not start with gratitude because that will stop the complaining. Then move optimism in to fill the void.
You will receive what you create.

Day 250

Give yourself to the river and He will take care of the rest.

*Life is like a river.
Better to go with the flow than swim against its natural direction.
You'll still end up in the sea whether or not you decide to fight against it.
This is to understand the nature of God who is the river.
Give yourself to the river and He will take care of the rest.*

Day 251

Celebrating each day as if the storm was over.

Have you ever noticed how a disaster, like a flood or a storm, brings local communities together.

Barriers start to break down and people are much more helpful and friendly to one another?

The barriers of hate and fear give way to love and compassion.
Celebrations can also have a similar effect such as the anniversary of the end of a war.
Isn't this bizarre to think it takes a catastrophe for us to behave in a way that should come naturally.
If we think about it, we could all live every day with love and compassion by celebrating life itself.

Day 252

Forgive yourself and all will become clear.

If you find your head is full of negative thoughts about other people making you feel stressed or upset, pause a while and think again.

*Where exactly is this stress or anxiety?
Is it out there where you think the affliction came form?
Are you saying that the other person or situation made you think in a negative way?
Or, is it something you created within your mind?
Once you realise that the negativity comes from within, start by taking back control of your mind by wanting to change, to be more positive and happy.
Now forgive yourself for this error in your thinking. Forget about the other person or situation, they moved on a long time ago. It no longer exists.
Forgive yourself and all will become calm and clear.*

Day 253

We live within the limits of a busy doctor.

I once went to the hospital with chest pains.

*The doctors were so busy ruling out heart problems that they overlooked to find out what the real problem was.
The pains went away and I was sent on my merry way the next day.
Are we not all in the same frame of mind as these doctors?
We are so habitually preoccupied with all things familiar that we overlook to take a fresh look at ourselves.
If we clear all our preconceptions, be still for a while, we might be able to diagnose our real state of well-being.*

Day 254

Life is like a dirty window.

*Life is like a dirty window,
We only realise how messy it has become after it has been cleaned.
Then you can see the difference.
Before then, we live in the dark.*

Day 255

The dawning of the dusk.

Have you ever wondered why everything appears to comes alive at dusk.
Sheep are baa-ing, birds are singing and yet all around appears calm.
For some reason, we humans have a heightened sense of awareness at dusk.
Things become clearer and there is an inner calm.
Perhaps as the mind sees the end of the day approaching it naturally quietens down for the day.
Only then can we see through the inner chatter and things become clearer.
Go out at dusk and experience it.

Day 256

Even though there will be temptation all around, be the shepherd of your thoughts.

*You are your own shepherd.
Your flock is the many aspects of the mind.
Sometimes they can stray off and get lost.
Don't hate your sheepish thoughts for this.
They do not know any better.
Just bring them back into the flock and keep a watchful eye for the next stray.
Even though there will be temptation all around, be the shepherd of your thoughts.*

Day 257

<u>You are what you think you are.</u>

*Close your eyes and remember the worse day of your life.
How do you feel?....pretty awful I imagine.
Now close your eyes again and imagine the best day of your life.
How do you feel?.... pretty joyful I*

imagine.
So, what's the difference? Nothing of course. You are still in the same room with the same mind and body.
It would appear the we have complete control over our feelings regardless of any outside influences.
Choose wisely and life could be wonderful.

Day 258

<u>A dream within a dream of dreams.</u>

Most of our lives are lived out in a dream state. And when you go to sleep you live out a dream within a dream.
Only when you can turn off the constant chatter in the mind can you wake up and get a glimpse of reality.
Only when you realise that you are the dreamer that you are able to conduct the dream to your own satisfaction.
Realise also that most other beings are dreaming out their dreams too.

Day 259

A worrying mind feeds on fear so by starving it, the worrying will let go.

Have you every been frustrated because you can't get something out of your mind like a song, or something that happened earlier that day or even worrying about the future?

Every time you block it out, it just comes straight back at you as soon as your back it turned. The more frustrated you get the more energy you give it and the more intense it becomes.

I've heard there's another way so let's try it.

Rather than turn your back on it, give it your full attention. Not blindly but with self-awareness. Observe it. Let it play itself out.

You might start noticing it becomes less intensive and more fragmented. Observe it, smile at it inwardly. Make

*friends with it.
It will suddenly disappear as it loses its grip on you. A worrying mind feeds on fear so by starving it, it will let go.*

Day 260

Thoughts can be like a propelled boat, parting through our sea of calmness. Causing separation.

*Think about what goes on in your mind, moment to moment.
Many would not even realise what is going on in that endless chatter.
Possibly a mischievous mind looking for advantages or trying to get ahead.
But your advantage is another person's disadvantage. Conflict and negative thoughts arise.
And so we live in a divided state of being.
Think of these thoughts as a propelled boat splicing through the water.
You are part of the water and so you*

become separated by its parting; divided.
You can make the boat go away any time you wish and make the division disappear.
Re-join the separation and be as One again in calmer waters.

Day 261

<u>Universal wisdom.</u>

Wisdom comes from all things.
We are all part of that wisdom.
You just need to know where to look.
And you will find it resting within.

Day 262

<u>Better to have a teacher who knows the way than to work it out for yourself.</u>

There are many paths to enlightenment. Buddhism, Christianity, Islam, Mindfulness,

Zen to name just a few.
Those that do not choose a path are still finding their way to betterment.
It is far better to have a teacher who knows the way than to try to work it out for yourself.

Day 263

Like passing ships on their way to eternity, we move on with fondness.

I have known people who have grieved daily over the loss of their loved ones.
Are they grieving for themselves, being left alone?.
This would seem to be a selfish act where the person focuses on their own loss and not so much on their partner.
If their partners could look upon them from heaven they would certainly not want their loved one to grieve.
And so there's a sense of irony with grief. Eventually you have to move on. We are all like passing ships on our way to

eternity.
Have fond memories but do not dwell in darkness.

Day 264

Life is like an mp3 player on shuffle.

Like an mp3 player on shuffle, life is an extravaganza of unpredictability and surprises.

Day 265

One another, as one.

Look at people without preconceived ideas,
Without a clouded mind,
But with a simpleness as if at one with the world.
From this, each individual becomes your family.
Each becomes your friend

*With rich understanding of one another
As one.*

Day 266

<u>Using a dream in order to awaken.</u>

*Try this.... See what you think.
Close your eyes.
Imagine a ball of dense grey smoke in front of you.
You're feeling like that smoke all heavy, tired and wasted.
You're too wasted to change but you're going to have to punch through the smoke to reach a better world, a world of light and joy.
Without any further hesitation, move fast into the smoke, as fast as you can and punch through with your whole being to the other side.
You made it!
Now you feel lighter, awakened and full of purpose.*

Day 267

Calmness will provide you with a clear reflection of yourself.

Just as when you look at your reflection on the water, you can only see a clear reflection of yourself if you remain calm for a while.

Day 268

Discovery that the farthest object is 13.4 billion light years away.

In 2016 scientists discovered the farthest thing in the universe; a galaxy that emitted light some 13.4 billion years ago. I wonder what that galaxy looks like now, some 13.4 billion years later
It casts doubts over what we think about the dawn of the universe because it should not exist and yet it does.

It seems that our discoveries are only limited by our capacity to perceive what is around us.
That we only perceive a tiny speck, smaller than an atom, in comparison to what else is out there that we cannot perceive.
How arrogant we seem, to think we know all there is to know, when all the time we Earth people know so little.

Day 269

After all of mankind's great discoveries there's still one thing left unchallenged.

Mankind has made great discoveries in the past few hundred years.
He has learnt to conquer whole continents, travel at high speeds on both land, sea and air, pioneered huge medical advances and created communication devices that would amaze all those that lived before.
Indeed, mankind has become so

*powerful he thinks he is God. In fact, he does not need God anymore as he thinks he has surpassed anything that God could offer.
And yet there's one thing that he has not yet conquered.
One thing as yet to be fully understood.
One thing left to be discovered.
That is....
Himself.*

Day 270

Rich Man - Poor Man. Which is which?

*Set yourself large goals and you will only ever achieve part of what you want in life and feel unfulfilled.
Set yourself small goals and you will always achieve what you want in life and feel fulfilled.*

Day 271

What if?

*What if all that fear, sorrow and pain goes away when we die.
What if when our bodies die our minds go on living.
What if the mind is our soul-spirit; part of a collective consciousness.
What if we do not have secret thoughts but these are all known to the collective consciousness.
What if our true selves are part of a Godlike energy that has no beginning or end but our minds on earth are incapable of comprehending this.
What if we have been such fools on earth to think we know everything and yet we know nothing.*

Day 272

All things are like the rain.

Do we get angry with the rain when it gets us wet?
Maybe. It depends on whether you like the rain or not.
Does the rain know if it causing you grief or joy?
Of course not. The rain just does its thing.
So it's not the rain that is different, it's your state of mind.
All things are like the rain.

Day 273

<u>The mindful garden.</u>

Look at your mind as if it is a garden. The bad thoughts are the weeds and the good thoughts are the flowers and shrubs.
As you would regularly tend to your garden, do so also with your mind by pulling out the bad thoughts (the weeds) and nurturing the good thoughts (the

flowers and shrubs).
That way you will have a beautiful mind.

Day 274

The scrap heap challenge of a busy mind.

Are you one of those with a busy mind? If you find yourself thinking wasteful thoughts that seem to do more harm than good then thinks again my friend. Think of these wasteful thoughts as waste indeed. A rubbish heap that keeps on building up and up until you do not see the light anymore and nothing grows. You build your own scrap heap of wasteful thinking.
Now let's think again. As with the natural environment, the less waste we produce the less we choke up the landscape within our minds.
So let's give ourselves a rest from producing wasteful thoughts and in the calmness, you will look around and see

*the reality you have been covering up.
A world of light, beauty and growth.*

Day 275

Collecting mental manacles.

*As we travel through life,
We pick up more and more mental baggage along the way.
Until it begins to slow us down so much,
We can barely think clearly to progress any further.
At this stage, life might seem intolerable.
So, what's there to do?
Well, shed the load of course.
Learn to let go.
You might feel a little scared at first as you will have this illusion that it's safer to have a burden than to let go.
Not so my friends. Try it for a day.
Regularly say, "I have let go of all my worries and wasteful thoughts".
You will see how much lighter the journey becomes.*

*Much more pleasant.
Joyful.*

Day 276

<u>Multiple choice question</u>

*Why do I exist?
Is it:
1 - I just do and that's it
2 - Life is a playground to be lived to the full.
3 - To master my ego through humility, compassion, calmness and mindfulness.
Answer.....
All of the above.
We are free to be our own creators of whatever we want out of life.*

Day 277

<u>You are your own shepherd.</u>

Why can't we just get through life without having to check ourselves about what we think, what we do or say? Here's why: For some reason we tend to stray from what is good for us, believing that the grass is greener on the other side. Always wanting more
Just as a lamb would stray from the flock, only to get lost in the wilderness.
So, we do need to keep ourselves in check regularly. Ask 'how am I doing?', 'is this where I want to be?', 'am I thinking straight?'.
Then you can herd yourself back into what you feel is right for you.

Day 278

Car - Body Maintenance

Just like a car that needs topping up with oil and water regularly, we too need regular maintenance to keep ourselves running properly.

*Our maintenance consists of having the right amount of food, warmth, exercise, relationships and compassion.
And then we're rearing to go!*

Day 279

<u>A momentous ocassion.</u>

*Be in the moment
and
the moment will be in you.*

Day 280

<u>Rome wasn't built in a day.</u>

*Just like a well-built house with a good foundation and solid brick walls,
You need to build a mind that is strong and sure in order to weather any storm that life throws at you.
How do you do this?
Brick by brick of course, in stages of*

*learning about your Self.
Rome wasn't built in a day.*

Day 281

You are your own barometer. Take a reading and act upon it.

*Have you ever asked yourself if you are following the right path on your journey through life?
Maybe not...maybe you just go with the flow.
But is that flow the right path for you?
How do you know?
By listening to yourself and being open to how you feel.
Say do I feel good about this?...do I feel bad about that?
And then act on it.
You are your own barometer. Take a reading and decide if you need to change in order to find sunshine in your life.*

Day 282

Practice makes perfect.

*When you start out each morning, think about what sort of day you would like for yourself.
You can choose.
Would you like a day of criticising people, including yourself and feel horrible as a result?
Or would you like to have a quiet peaceful mind and enjoy the day from moment to moment?
Then, constantly remind yourself when you need to think or act, is this going to help me achieve what I have chosen for myself?
Keep making that decision throughout your day as thoughts and situations arise.
You will start to be what you desire.*

Day 283

A poor man that is rich - A rich man that is poor.

*A man that is wealthy in spirit is a wealthy man indeed.
A man that is poor in health but with plenty of money is a poor man in need.
A man full of love for his fellow man will surely succeed.
A man that cares not for anybody, then his heart will surely bleed.*

Day 284

Is your life a comedy of errors?

*We are the characters in our own play.
The play is called Life.
I urge you to write the script in the way you want it to be.*

*You are not part of someone else's play.
That would be a comedy of errors.*

Day 285

<u>**An answer without a question is surely a nonsense.**</u>

*Listen to the ramblings of the mind.
Maybe you are replaying a situation that happened recently.
Why would you do this?.
To search for a solution in there somewhere.
An answer to a question.
Stop for a moment.
Ask yourself, what is the question?
You are looking for an answer for which you have not identified the question.
An answer without a question is surely a nonsense.
Until you realise this you will continue to ramble.*

Day 286

The complexities of trouble and strife (life) boil down to one thing.

All your problems in life boil down to one thing.
Just one problem...not many.
One veil...not many.
One.

Day 287

We are but children, playing out a game of life.

We are but like children with toys to play with.
We want to play imaginary games with our lives.
We often sit back and watch others do

this on the television.
Is this detachment from reality not the cause of our discontent?
To imagine we are something we are not.
Let's start by realising this; that the game of life is but just a game.
We've all been played at our own game.

Day 288

<u>**Nature has no self-imposed rules like mankind has.**</u>

Do you feel stuck in a rut with your 9 to 5 job and not enough hours in the day?
Think about this for a moment. These are your man-made rules that you are working to.
A bird that flies freely in the sky does not work to these rules.
A fish swimming in the ocean does not work to these rules.
A squirrel living in the trees does not work to these rules.
Animals do not work to self-made rules

*and yet I've never seen a miserable animal in the wild.
I've seen miserable animals in zoos that live by man's rule of captivity.
So we have a lot to learn from nature if we want to live in reality; not to put ourselves in a zoo cage, but be free, be happy.*

Day 289

Be the king of your kingdom, the master of your house.

*You can be a king, a queen, a president, prime minister or a world leader.
This you can achieve in just a fleeting moment.
That is...you can be a leader of your world.
Your world is within you, not externally.
All that you perceive is experienced from within.
So don't let your mind be unruly...rule it.
Be the king of your kingdom.*

Day 290

Our friend the moon, as a reminder of our understanding of all things.

Last night I looked up at the beautiful moon, big and round in the low sky, set behind a layer of thin streaky cloud. All seemed still. It was inspiring.
I then realised that the whole of the moon is always there, even when it appears as a thin slither of a crescent.
We seem to think that only part of the moon exists when it is like this because we cannot see the rest, which is in darkness.
This is surely a reflection of our understanding of all things.
We think we know all there is to know and yet in reality, we only see what has been lit up for us by our senses and our sense of reason.
How much more of this universe there is, we will never know, until the whole is

revealed to us.
So when you next look up at the crescent moon. Remind yourself that this is so much more to life that cannot be seen.

Day 291

<u>*As they say...forgive and forget*</u>

There are two types of forgiveness where you can either say:

I forgive you but don't do it again as I am better than you. Let's move on but I am right and you are wrong.
I forgive you, but most of all I forgive myself for thinking that I am better than you and bringing in hate and fear to the situation. Let's move on as equals. There is nothing to forgive.
Which one would you choose? Which one would make you feel good about yourself?

Day 292

What can you gain by letting go? Everything.

*The ego mind is dependent on external influences to make everything right.
Only you can decide if this is what you want.
You can go back to sleep and let the ego mind take over.
Or you can wake up and be the master of your ego.
The result is that you will not need to rely on external influences for happiness.
So, you gain happiness by letting go the e-go.*

Day 293

Being human.

We are all human beings.

So why don't we try being human

...and not something else.

Day 294

Life through a rear view mirror.

*Do not run your life like a driver looking through the rear-view mirror.
Don't look at what has past.
Look ahead, otherwise you will surely crash.*

Day 295

A simple exercise before you get up in a morning.

*The minute you awaken, catch yourself before slipping into busy mind mode.
Relax and move around to get rid of any tension in the body.
Breath and feel the air gently passing through your nostrils.*

Now, scan your whole body starting from your feet, working your way up both legs to your thighs, belly, chest, back.
Then moving up from your fingertips, hands, arms and shoulders.
If you struggle to focus, count down from 10 slowly whilst continuing to breath and feel the presence of your body.
Working up through your neck, cheeks, nose, ears, eyes, forehead and your crown.
Now take in the whole of your body as one, ensure it feels relaxed and heavy.
Keep a clear mind and enjoy the calm and peacefulness.
You are now ready to get up and start your day.
Maintain that feeling and feel in control.

Day 296

An owed ode that must be showed.

*As you travel through life,
Down that bumpy road.
Following strife
Until your brain starts to corrode.
Learn to let go,
Lighten your load.
Be in the flow,
In a heavenly abode.*

Day 297

What love is not, is not love.

*What is love?
We can talk all day about what love is not.
Maybe a 1,000-page book that would take a year to read and understand.
Our lives are so full of non-love in all its complexities that it becomes an ongoing circle of mind chatter.
STOP - SWITCH OFF - LET GO.
Pause in silence for a while.
Love was there all along, shining on me*

*and you.
Peaceful, smiling, cheerful and kind.*

Day 298

Bring your umbrella down and feel the rain.

*Love rains down on all the universe.
Including all mankind.
So, bring down your umbrella
And feel the rain of love.*

Day 299

Smile and the whole world smiles with you.

*Quick, from 1 to 10 how do you feel, 1 being terrible, 10 being incredible.
Just for fun, why not send signals to the brain that your body is happy.
Lift the edges of your lips upwardly....that's it keep going.*

*It may seem more strenuous for some than others,
Like having 5kg weights tied to the corners of our mouth.
There you go...
So , what's your score now?
More?
So you do have control over your happiness after all.*

Day 300

In search of truth.

*What complex lives we lead in search of something that just never seems to materialise.
We hardly know what it is we are searching for, only that we need to work hard and play hard to achieve this something.
My friend, realise that it is the truth you are searching for and you already have it within you.
So no need to be hard on yourself and*

enjoy the peace and happiness that comes with this knowing.

Day 301

Be true to yourself. Less is more.

*I believe that we should focus on knowing ourselves before we go forth into the world chasing our ambitions.
Focus on being true to yourself and others, live in peace, be kind, steady and sure.
All else will fall into place without having to prove yourself to anyone.
This is hard since we have not been taught that less is more.*

Day 302

Letting our egos rule, whilst cleverly masking our arrogance.

*The human race has concepts about all things, whether animate or inanimate.
Even concepts about concepts, such as opinions, sometimes leading to judgements.
So after a lifetime of conceptualising, do we feel we are getting somewhere in knowing all there is?
No, there's still a sense that there's more, almost like a restless caged animal that can't stop pacing up and down.
Stop pacing for a while and ask, where is this leading us?
Is it to achieve ultimate knowledge and understanding of all things?
Is it to say, God is dead, we are better than God.
We let our egos rule, whilst cleverly masking our arrogance.
True understanding is already with you, from within.*

Day 303

Our nameless universe.

For we humans, everything we see and everything we discover has to be given a name.
Sure, this helps to communicate the world we live in to each other.
But this is only limited to the human experience of which we are only 1 of 8.7 billion species living on planet earth.
In reality, nothing has a name. Nothing in the entire universe.
It just is.

Day 304

Pause for thought in our daily lives.

In your daily routine,
Stop for a while.
Switch off your 'machine',
And give a little smile.
Be quiet in mind,
And think of your health.

*For what you will find,
Is your true Self.*

Day 305

<u>*You are whatever you focus on.*</u>

*You become whatever you focus on.
If you criticise and judge, then you will live a life of criticisms and judgements.
If you live in fear then you will either put yourself down or be aggressive towards others.
If you watch a lot of violence on the television then your mind will either be secretly or openly violent in nature.
All these illusions being played out by the mind.
Why not try love, peace and happiness towards yourself and others, instead?
So, that you become whatever you focus on.*

Day 306

Big or small...be grateful for what you have and be humble.

*Be grateful for whatever you have in life. There are thousands of children dying of starvation and homeless in the world so whatever problems you think you have, think again.
Be humble and savour your good fortune, however big or small.*

Day 307

Live and let live.

*Do not force your concepts of how to live onto others.
They will have their own ideas that will equally work for them.
If you find common ground that is a bonus.
Show respect whilst keeping the 'door*

*open'.
Above all, live and let live.*

Day 308

<u>Drop, Stop and Swap...Beyond words.</u>

*Have you ever thought about truly listening to someone speak to you?.
This might sound obvious but usually we go about our business without paying much attention to what is being said.
Three things:*

*Drop all chatter in the mind.
Stop all preconceptions.
Swap mindlessness for mindful listening.*

True understanding is beyond words.

Day 309

Medicines help us to live unhealthy lifestyles.

Despite modern advances in medicine some of the best cures are either free or cost next to nothing.

For example, walking amongst nature, laughter, having a friendly chat, gentle touch, water, eating fresh fruit and salad...

Instead, we watch too much television, fear failure in our society, drink alcohol, smoke and eat carcinogenic foods.

It seems that medicines are there to save us from ourselves. Which allows us to continue to live an unhealthy lifestyle.

Day 310

We are all connected. We are all one.

Don't be tempted to judge or criticise anyone.
We are all connected as one.

*So if you do verbal harm to another, you are doing it to yourself.
Even if you do it secretly within your mind.
Think about it. How does it make you feel.
Any satisfaction is short lived and leaves you feeling negative.
We are all One.*

Day 311

From destruction to construction.

*Often in our society innocence is seen as a sign of weakness.
Especially when you reach adulthood.
You fall easy prey to those that are looking to hide their insecurity by attacking you.
That in turn leads to the innocent becoming protective by either withdrawing or becoming another attacker.
A sea of change is require to nurture innocence based on knowledge, understanding and equality.*

*After all, innocence is where we all originate.
This will change the destructive cycle into a constructive cycle.*

Day 312

The activity of the mind enshrouds our true nature.

*We who live by the activity of the mind no longer see our true nature.
Be still for a while and realise that what seems like a fleeting glimpse of something lovely is in fact an awakening to our true selves.*

Day 313

Realise that your true self is eternal.

*We fear death so much that it seems taboo to talk about it.
And yet it is the one thing in life that is*

certain.
Take comfort that there is a higher order at work here.
That death is just a fleeting transition back to our true selves.
Dispel any fear as it will prevent you from living life to the full.
Realise your true self in each moment.
That you are eternal.

Day 314

Take off your mask and stop pretending.

Do you identify yourself with a type of person?
For example, I am an accountant, I am a shopkeeper, I am an ex-soldier, I am aggressive, I am weak, I have low self-esteem.
All these labels for what we think we are can take us over, leaving us fixated on an illusory idea to the exclusion of the rest of the world, leaving us empty when an inevitable change comes along.

Take off this mask and see yourself as nobody. Learn to let go. You will then become more aware of the world and discover who you really are.

Day 315

<u>The ego mind is wild and on the loose.</u>

*The ego is like a wild animal.
In our modern world it has become confused.
Thus, it has become unruly in its bid to make sense of it all.
It needs some attention, some guidance and looking after.
So don't try to ensnare the wild animal and try to cage it.
Make it your pet, stroke it; it can be tamed.
After all, you are its owner.*

Day 316

Look at the heart of another and you will see a part of yourself.

The heart is where we feel compassion, which is like a mirror.
Once you see the heart of another person, it will reflect its image of yourself.

Day 317

Judgement bounces back like a rubber ball against brick wall.

To judge another leaves you feeling judged.

Day 318

Who are you? Answer...not what you think.

When you look at a person what do you see.
Do you see a memory of what they did

yesterday?
Do you see them as a threat?
Do you criticise them for their appearance?
Or do you see them as an object of desire?
All these ideas made within the mind, but which one is true?
Answer....none of them.
Instead, look at them as if for the first time without preconceived ideas.
You will see the real person and there will be no more conflict.

Day 319

<u>The game of life.</u>

The game of life often reflects love and fear.
Roll the dice and see what you land on next.
There's only one winner to several losers.
Winning or losing is not important.
The important thing is to realise it is just a

game, so follow your path and enjoy taking part.

Day 320

A reminder to live in the moment.

Many of us live out our lives inside our minds, full of ideas, loves and hates. We live in the past, in the future, in a kind of self-made hell at its extremes. Alternatively, we can wake up out of this daydream and live in the moment. Each and every instant without interference from the mindless chatter. To live in the 'now' is to wake up to reality. We have a choice to make. Make it now! In every moment.

Day 321

Even a prisoner can be free.

A prisoner that is unaffected by the world, who is not vulnerable to influences in the prison and rests in confidence without swaying, is truly free.

Day 322

<u>Rungs of wisdom - Part 1</u>

Words of wisdom are merely rungs of a ladder that help you step up to a higher place. When you arrive, you no longer need the rungs of wisdom unless you go back down to help guide others take those steps.

Day 323

<u>Rungs of wisdom - Part 2</u>

When you have climbed up the wisdom ladder to that higher place you will say to yourself, 'Its not much fun on my own and

besides, whilst I see others lower down the ladder, I do not feel content or whole'.
So you go back down to help people up. Because of this, you cannot achieve full wisdom until everyone is with you in that higher place.

Day 324

Every day is a new adventure.

Someone said over the radio today, 'What will you do today that you have never done before?'.
It could have been going skiing, doing a bungee jump or eating sprouts (!).
My answer is 'Everything'.
None of us have lived today before, nor will we live it again. Every day is unique. So if you are bored with life and feel you need to do something different, think again.
Wake up and realise that in every moment, you already are.

Day 325

When you forgive, don't forget to forgive and forget.

*Understand why you would forgive somebody that has offended you.
It's not about the other person at all.
It's about you.
Unless you forgive you will carry that wrongdoing with you long after it happened.
Then afterwards, you continue to do it to yourself, over and over in your mind.
So, forgive and move on.*

Day 326

Live for the moment, without the fusion of confusion in illusion.

If I live in the moment, I do away with all those worries and fears about being on

*time for the next part of my life.
All I know is The Now.
It doesn't mean I do not care about when I arrive at an appointed time. I still do the things required to live a full and meaningful life.
However, it does mean that I will enjoy whatever I do without the confusion of illusion, from moment to moment, regardless of the circumstances.*

Day 327

Teachers are like mirrors. We are all teachers.

*Teachers are like mirrors.
They mirror an image of the truth.
We are all like mirrors
We are all like teachers.
Reflecting the truth.
Not the real truth.
But the truth according to our own experience.*

Day 328

Doing nothing to achieve something.

Cultivating a quiet mind helps us to see more clearly.
Cultivating a quiet mind can be hard to do.
It requires you to stop trying.
It requires no effort.
Not to do.
Just be.
Be.

Day 329

A bad workman blames his tools.

They say a bad workman blames his tools.
That is to say, when things go wrong, we look beyond ourselves for reasons why and judge it or blame it.

*So we never get to see that it is our own perception that went wrong.
And we never get to say, 'Don't judge it but learn from it and move on', because we are always looking elsewhere, outside ourselves.*

Day 330

Realise that your reality is not real.

*Are we capable of experiencing true reality?
We rely on our 5 senses to receive reality within the world around us.
We then hope that the brain will receive this reality and interpret it correctly for us.
We also assume there is nothing else out there that our senses cannot pickup.
We're all different so we all have our own versions of this reality.
True reality is therefore not what we perceive.
That's ok.... just enjoy the show.*

Day 331

There's a whole lot of reality going on.

Your reality is individual to yourself.
There are 7 billion people living on this planet.
Therefore, there are 7 billion realities.

Day 332

All around and all within.

All around you there is creation dazzling.
The universe is ever changing.
All within you there is creation happening.
The inner universe is rearranging.

Day 333

What a wonderful life, to decide whether or not we wish to be ill.

I've heard that most, if not all, illnesses are a result of our own decisions.
So that would imply we have complete power over our own bodies.
Makes sense I guess.... after all they are ours to choose whatever we want during our body's life span.
If you do not believe this then it is not going to be.
If you do, and fully understand it's meaning, then what a wonderful life it is indeed.

Day 334

The sea of life.

Like waves rolling in from the sea,
True knowledge washes over us in waves.
It ebbs and flows like the tide.

*Until one day we get washed out to sea
And join that great ocean.*

Day 335

<u>A most compelling choice.</u>

*What is your body?.
Is it you...the self?
If so, then you will die eventually and cease to exist.
Our strong sense of survival makes us question this.
Is the body something we occupy for a while?
If so, then our true selves, our consciousness, will eventually leave our bodies.
Maybe go back to whence we came.
Maybe an eternity of peace and bliss.
We may not have much evidence but it is a most compelling belief.
If one of these options worries you then why not go with the one that makes you the happiest.*

Day 336

Ignorance is about ignoring the news. About being blissful.

*They say that 'Ignorance is bliss'.
And yet we insist on watching the daily news that only wants to report bad things that happen in the world. This seems to be designed to stir our emotions, make us feel bad about ourselves and the world around us.
So yes, ignorance is bliss.*

Day 337

Get rid of the root cause and not the effects.

*Our daily lives are full of negative thoughts, judgements and doubts.
It becomes habitual to the point we think it is normal.*

*Each negative thought is like a weed that keeps growing back even if we try chopping bits back.
The only way to rid yourself of this is to uproot the weed, remove the whole habitual thought process, and throw it in the bin.*

Day 338

Opening the gateway through daily practice.

*Bring your awareness to the present moment.
Focus on the breath.
Stop the mind's chatter by realising it is not real.
Stop all beliefs by realising they are incorrect interpretations.
This will open the gateway to much more peace and understanding.
Less is more.*

Day 339

The stepping stones to truth and happiness.

There's a lot of literature and videos out there that teaches us mindfulness and how to live in the moment.
We can become experts at it and yet at the same time still feel like we are not getting anywhere.
Only when we put the book down and switch the video off will we truly achieve what we are looking for.
The theory is but a stepping stone to true happiness.

Day 340

Life is but a mirror of your mind.

*The quality of life much depends on the quality of the mind.
Everything else is irrelevant.*

Day 341

<u>Is being wise, the ability to judge right from wrong?.</u>

*What is wisdom?
Is it the ability to judge something between right and wrong?.
But if you do this you are saying that you know what's best and your judgement is universally accepted by all. You're saying you are as good as God.
If you think this then you are deluding yourself and therefore not capable of wisdom.
So, it stands to reason that true wisdom includes the ability to see all things without judgement.*

Day 342

All aboard the train journey of a lifetime.

*Our life on earth is like a train journey.
It has both a departure and arrival time and place.
Once we get going there's a whole lot of world to see through the windows of our mind.
But most of us tend to sleep through the journey and miss the full experience.
Let's wake up and enjoy the ride!*

Day 343

Leadership without the game of politics.

*Politics is no longer about debate, it's about mind games.
There's no doubt that all around the world there are political games being played out both within each country's politicians and between world leaders.
This is fuelled by the mass media wanting*

to grab a good story, whether it's true or speculative.
They use the term 'political football' when we see issues being kicked around, for personal goals, leaving winners and losers.
It's a form of road rage whereby everybody involved feels aggrieved.
Is this appearance of our outer world not a reflection of the turmoil going on in our inner world; our minds?
So, to bring some sanity into our outer world we first need to calm our minds, bring some sanity back by not playing the political mind games (even secretly to ourselves).
If enough people stop the mind politics within themselves then eventually the outer world will mirror this.
World leaders could be appointed on how much they meditate and the calmness of their minds, which promotes clarity of thought and compassion for all.
If you scoff at this idea then you are addicted to turmoil.

Day 344

Focus, be steady and the path will open itself to you.

How can you follow the path to happiness if you're not focussing on where you are going?
You'll be full of life's distractions, keep bumping into things and going the wrong way.
Better to focus, no?

Day 345

Which 'F' word will you choose?

Two 'F' words to choose from:
Fear or Forgiveness.
Through our eyes of perception, we can see the world either in fear or in forgiveness.
What's your preference?

Day 346

Wondering lonely as a cloud in a crowd.

The loneliest place to live on this planet is within a highly populated city.
All those people and yet no one to talk to. No one who'll listen.
Now that's a funny thing.
We are an odd bunch, we humans.

Day 347

What gets bigger as you use it up?

The wonderful thing about being creative is the more you create, the more creativity you have.
Nothing gets used up. It just keeps growing.
Don't let your thinking limit you.
Just be creative.

Day 348

Children are our teachers. The origins of adulthood.

*Some of our greatest teachers are children.
They unveil the source of our way of thinking.
Jealousy, envy, loves and hates can be observed in children.
It can stay with us for many years beyond childhood.
Are we not but children in our minds?
Maybe it's time we grew (up).*

Day 349

Meaning of prodigal: Wasteful, self-indulgent, reckless...

*We are all prodigal sons.
We have left our spiritual home.*

*Our home is our sense of joy and love for self and others.
We have forgotten our true nature within the universe.
As with the biblical story, we can come home any time and all is forgiven.
Do we need to fall on hard times in order to turn back?
No, of course not. Home is always there to welcome us, to visit for a while and to stay.*

Day 350

<u>Once we have learnt the truth, we can then learn to let go of what we learnt.</u>

*Why do we seek the help of others in order to learn the truth?
As with a broken leg, it needs support to help it mend.
But as the repair becomes complete (and we return to the truth),*

we then need to let go and 'stand on our own two feet'.

Day 351

<u>Post trauma of everyday life.</u>

*When soldiers come out of battle they can suffer post trauma.
They find it difficult to put down their weapons and get used to no longer being in the fight.
Some things leave a very deep footprint that are difficult to brush away.
This can happen in our day-to-day routine.
Our fight might have been disagreeing with someone, they might hurt you with what they say, or you feel aggrieved by the way a discussion went.
Later, you are still reliving that moment just as a soldier suffers from post trauma.
We think we can resolved this by fighting our way through it in our minds but it just keeps on coming back.*

*So, what is there to do with this ongoing worrying, reliving the past.
Realise you can't fight what is not real. you just go around in circles.
Put down your metaphorical weapons. Lighten your load. They are not real. They are imaginings; illusions. Leave them at the epitaph, say a prayer of forgiveness and walk away.
Above all forgive, forgive, forgive.... both yourself and your enemy.
Forgive you enemy and forgive yourself as you both did not know what you were doing.*

Day 352

The conclusion of our delusion needs a solution through inward revolution.

*You are influenced by everything that has gone before.
Your hairstyle, the way you dress, your interests, likes and dislikes...
With ongoing comparison and judging;*

*fear of non-conformity.
This conditioning has made you what you are today.
Maybe it's time for an inward revolution.*

Day 353

We are always at the tip of our evolution.

*Step out of your little world for a while and remember who you are.
You are the culmination of all events that have gone on before.
The tip of mankind's evolution.
It does not stop.
As time waits for no one.*

Day 354

A technological paradox.

*What has the mind of mankind created that is vastly superior to the human mind?
What have we created using our thought*

*processes so that we no longer have to use our thought processes?
What have we designed through hard work so that we no longer have to do hard work?
What is it that we fed all the answers so we don't have to work out the answers for ourselves?
Answer: I don't know, I'll have to Google it on my computer.*

Day 355

<u>Belief: Acceptance of a truth, without any proof.</u>

*Is it good to believe in something?
Do you have a belief in God?
Once you have that belief you are acknowledging that you have not attained what you believe in; that it is something not of today but of some future time to attain.
Does the belief actually have value...does it solve all your problems?*

No?
So having a belief creates a system of thought rather than the thing itself.
It creates confinement of which there is no escape whilst you believe.
Once you bring down the walls and stop believing, you become free.
You are then free to live your life as it should be.

Day 356

<u>Who is your ruler?</u>

Rule with the heart and not the brain.
The brain tries to create eternity.
The heart realises it is already in eternity.

Day 357

<u>I am; therefore I exist.</u>

*Like a computer, our minds are programmed by all the influences that we experience throughout our lives.
Both are mechanical or biological interactions of cause and effect.
However, unlike a computer we can say 'I am, therefore I exist'.
Is this not an acknowledgement that there is something higher at play here?*

Day 358

The blossom of being.

*If I water a plant it will blossom and most likely create a most beautiful flower.
In the same way, if we nurture our sense of integrity, love and compassion, we will blossom into a being of radiance.
As with the flower, the beauty and the radiance is there to behold by all those who open their eyes and see.*

Day 359

Tuning into the right frequency.

*If you want to receive a radio channel, you have to tune into it.
If you feel that you are living in fear, worry and aggression, it's because you are tuning into it. Could be the television, news or people around you.
If you want to receive peace, love and joy, again tune into it. Could be by meditation, being with nature or having loving friends.*

Day 360

Looking at a dusty mirror at dusty myself.

*Do you have a low opinion of yourself or suffer from low self-esteem?
Think about it, is your view of yourself real?
Could be that you've let too much dust gather on the mirror of your mind.*

*Rather than see your true self, you think you are the dust.
Clear your mind through having a quiet mind and you will see the real you.
The real you is divine and you will have no choice but to love what you see.*

Day 361

<u>Mindfulness - Being the observer.</u>

*Is meditation sitting on a cushion for hours on end trying to calm your mind?
You will most likely become frustrated as the mind wants to busy itself.
Or you will simply fall asleep, which is ok if you're tired.
No, actually you can meditate throughout your day doing whatever you need to do.
It's called Mindfulness. It's about being the observer.
Being aware of your body, mind and everything around you whilst keeping*

*your mind centered.
It helps to smile too.*

Day 362

You can still be the master of your ship without having the snip(!)

*I used to think that to become truly enlightened, one would have to change one's lifestyle...become a monk, say. The problem with that is most of us would like to become enlightened but not many of us would want to be a monk.
So what is the answer?
It's a matter of continuing with our daily lives but changing our perception of things from within. With more compassion.
Be the master of your ship and you will be able to steer through both calm and stormy waters.*

Day 363

The world is flat and time does exist?

*There's is a new school of thought that says time does not exist.
If this is true then all things are happening simultaneously.
The universe beyond the physical is therefore not governed by time.
It is being created on-mass. It is, all at once.
Our minds find it difficult to comprehend this but at least we no longer put people in jail for thinking the world is round (Galileo - 1633).*

Day 364

Good grounding - God founding.

Just as a building needs a strong foundation so that it does not topple, human beings also need a good foundation in knowledge and wisdom to

get through life.
Surrender to the grace of God and the foundation will be revealed to you.

Day 365

<u>Wizzing our way to true being.</u>

WizzWords...oh these words of wisdom,
Are but symbols of true seeing.
They are a mirror vision,
Not needed when we're being.

THE END

Printed in Great Britain
by Amazon